TALK WITH YOUR HANDS

TALK WITH

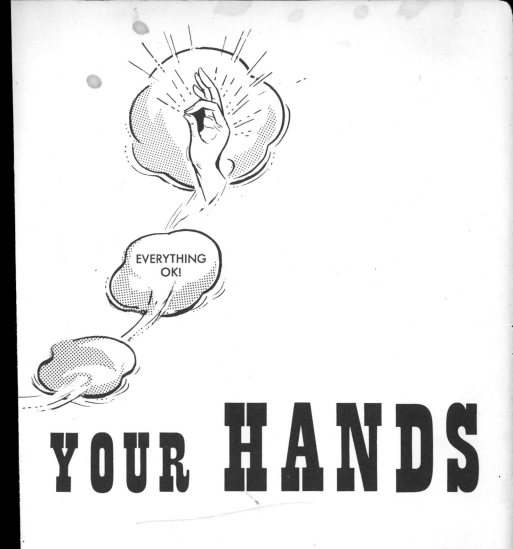

EVERYTHING OK!

YOUR HANDS

WRITTEN AND ILLUSTRATED BY

David O. Watson

Winneconne, Wisconsin

Foreword

Signs and gestures of one kind or another have been used since the beginning of time as a means of communication, to give emphasis to the spoken word, or to express a thought or feeling where the spoken word is found wanting.

An infant cries to attract attention, and he also kicks and waves his arms and smiles or frowns. When persons who speak different languages are drawn together they resort to gestures with their hands. In sports contests and dramatic performances instructions and signals are given by hand. On a signal from a coach, a baseball player attempts to steal a base and the umpire shows by gesture whether he is "safe" or "out." Dogs in the motion pictures are put through their paces by hand signals, for an audible command would find its way on to the sound track. There is a sign language even in nature, understood by both animals and men. A black cloud in the sky may be a "sign of rain."

So signs are a universal language. The American Indians used a highly developed system of signs. The deaf use a still more highly developed system, which is a language in itself. This book presents the sign language used by the deaf of America. It was originally brought to the United States from France, since education of the deaf in America originally was based upon the methods employed in France.

The deaf of this country are educated and well able to converse in the English language. Many are good lipreaders and they possess intelligible if not completely natural speech, but the sign language is the language they use most commonly in conversation among themselves, in their church services and in their parliamentary deliberations, because it is the most fluent means of communication for them. They appreciate it when their relatives and friends learn to use it, and talk to them on their hands.

Mr. Watson is well qualified to compile a book on the sign language. A son of deaf parents, he has used the sign language all his life. In this book he has devised a method of presentation which comes closest of any yet published to teach the reader to form the signs correctly and accurately. The best way to learn the sign language, of course, is to become acquainted with persons who use it and "learn by doing," but this book will provide an excellent foundation for any beginner, or for anyone who is not in constant association with the deaf.

Even those who are not in position to converse with the deaf will find it interesting. It will give them an additional means of communication which they will enjoy using, just for the fun of it.

BYRON B. BURNES, Litt. D.
President, National Association
of the Deaf.

Berkeley, California,
September 9, 1963.

v

CONTENTS

Introduction

The language of signs is a beautiful, graceful, and expressive art of communication. It is probably the easiest of the "foreign" languages to learn. The sky is the limit as to what the eloquence of your hands can do for you, once you have mastered the signs, in communicating your thoughts to another person (or an audience of many persons) fluently and meaningfully. It provides the "break-through" in its magical power to bring members of the family, relatives, and friends closer together. As exchanged thoughts are understood there also glow undestanding, love, joy, and fellowship.

There has been a long, urgent need for a book which would make it simple for anyone to learn to use the language of the signs. For this reason this book was designed in an entirely new presentation, executed in the simplest and most direct method of pictorial line drawing, so that the "arrested" motion in print can be learned with a glance, understood and repeated by anyone who knows nothing about the signs.

Before attempting to learn the signs, the reader is advised to begin by learning the manual alphabet (or fingerspelling) as presented on page 185. Here you will find complete instruction on how to form the letters on your hand. The drawings were prepared in two different views, to make it easier to master them. You will soon be able to fingerspell words and phrases rapidly and accurately. The reader will also observe throughout the book many words spelled out on the fingers. Many words have no known signs to designate them. They are presented to show how they can be used in combination with other signs to form phrases or sentences.

Samples of conversational sign language are used in the last part of our book, featured by a few of our own make-believe characters in adventurous comical situations. It is believed this is the first attempt ever made to illustrate in the printed form conversation as normally used by deaf persons everywhere. They also show how a correct English sequence can be used in sign conversation.

It is hoped that a better understanding between the general public and the deaf can be generated from this book. The signs shown here can be used in any situation in life. Deaf children will value the book as a textbook and their most prized possession. Relatives, friends, students, seminarians, priests, pastors, and welfare workers will likewise gain from it.

During the course of preparing this book, it was my privilege to come into contact with many persons including educators and deaf leaders, and I am thankful to them all, who displayed a helpful interest. Among them I feel that I must mention Dr. Elizabeth Benson, Dean of Women at Gallaudet College, a noted authority on the sign language, and Mr. John A. Gough, Director of Captioned Films for the Deaf in the U.S. Office of Education.

Dr. David Peikoff, Director of the Gallaudet College Centennial Fund offered advice and encouragement which were an inspiration to me through many difficult hours. Mrs. Renee Roles, Office Manager in the office of the National Association of the Deaf, rendered valuable assistance in typing and preparing the material.

I am especially grateful and indebted to my old friend, Dr. Byron B. Burnes, President of the National Association of the Deaf, for help with the organization of the material. He examined the original drawings on numerous occasions, offering helpful criticism, and he assisted with the preparation of the captions. His wife, Caroline H. Burnes, also contributed many valuable suggestions, which I appreciate.

Finally, my heartfelt thanks are hereby expressed to my sister, Angela Watson, whose encouragement, enthusiasm, and faith kept me going when at times the task seemed overwhelming; and to my wife, Beatrice, and our children, David P., Starr Lea, Arthur T., and Tracy Ann, who were denied certain pleasures and were at times practically abandoned while I confined my efforts to the completion of this book.

DAVID O. WATSON

HOW TO READ, UNDERSTAND, AND REPEAT THE "ARRESTED" MOTION IN PRINT

PLAYING CARDS

(4)

(2)

(1)

(Any kind of card game is indicated by the motion of dealing the cards.)

(3)

(2)

There are a few "keys" to remember before the reader starts flipping through these pages. Most important of all is to watch the position of the hands (1). Compare your hands with the drawing. The dotted hand is your first position before the movement begins.

The movement or direction of the hand (or hands) is indicated by the red line (2). The solid red arrow (3) means only one motion is required. Thus, the card dealer deals only once if one card is asked for. The open-faced or three-sided arrow (4) indicates the motion is to be repeated two or three times . . . several cards are dealt.

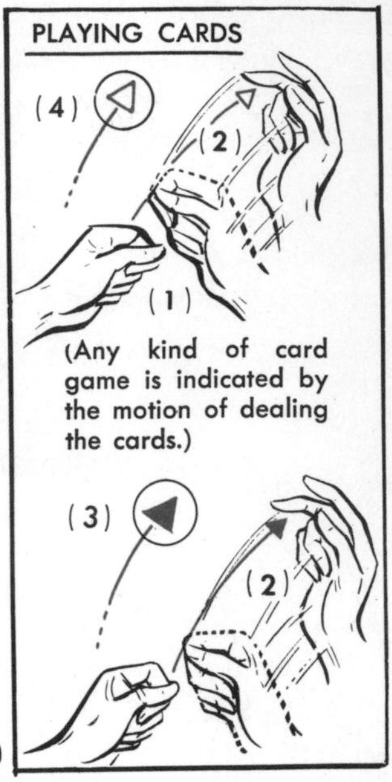

Compare the two illustrations below. The little finger dipping in the closed hand represents a brush or pen in an inkwell. Next, as seen here by the red line and solid red arrow, the hand is brought up to the "sketch pad". This is followed with a few strokes with the little finger on the "pad" as indicated by the open-faced arrow.

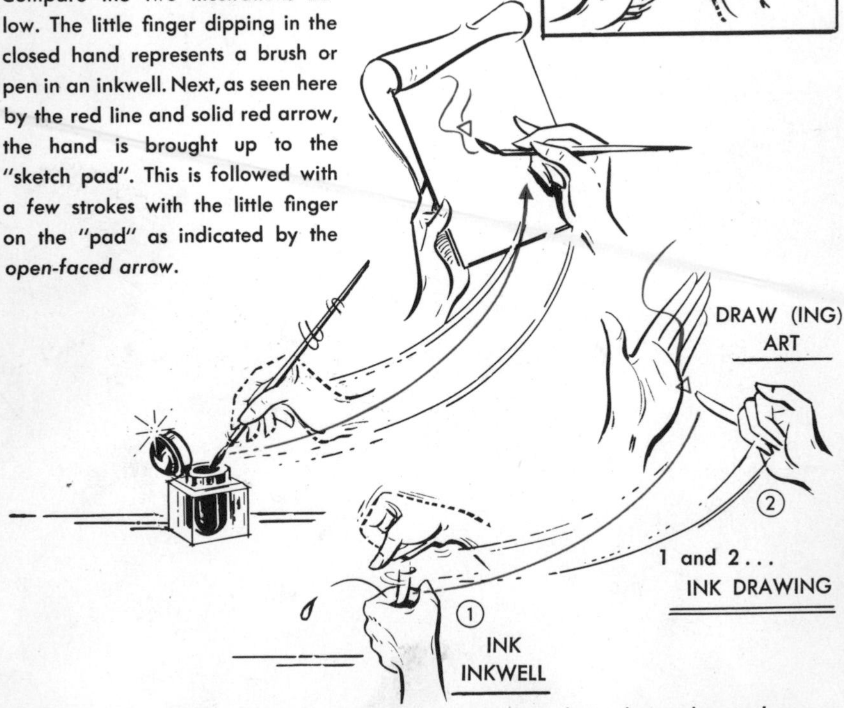

DRAW (ING) ART

INK INKWELL

1 and 2 . . . INK DRAWING

The circled numbers mean the combined signs are made in that order; and combining the two signs expresses the word or idea, "ink drawing". Sometimes a combination of three signs is formed to express an idea.

x

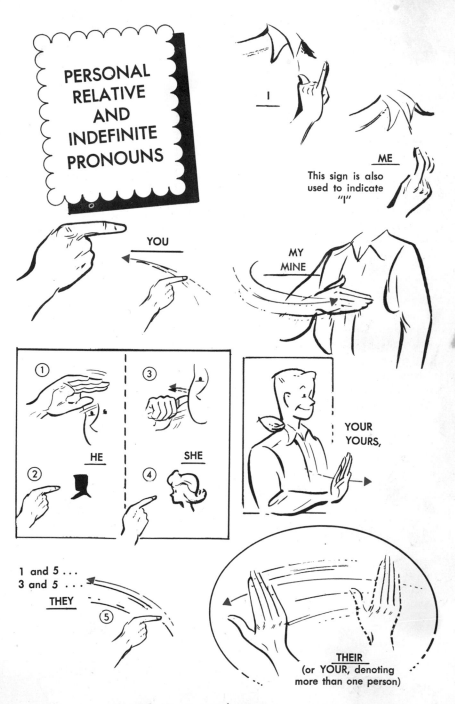

PERSONAL RELATIVE AND INDEFINITE PRONOUNS

I

ME

This sign is also used to indicate "I"

YOU

MY MINE

① HE

②

③ SHE

④

YOUR YOURS,

1 and 5 . . .
3 and 5 . . .
THEY
⑤

THEIR
(or YOUR, denoting more than one person)

1

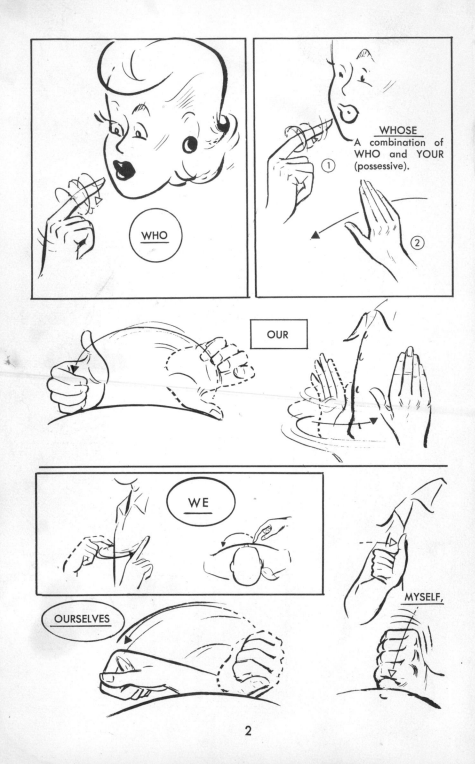

WHO

WHOSE
A combination of
WHO and YOUR
(possessive).

OUR

WE

OURSELVES

MYSELF,

2

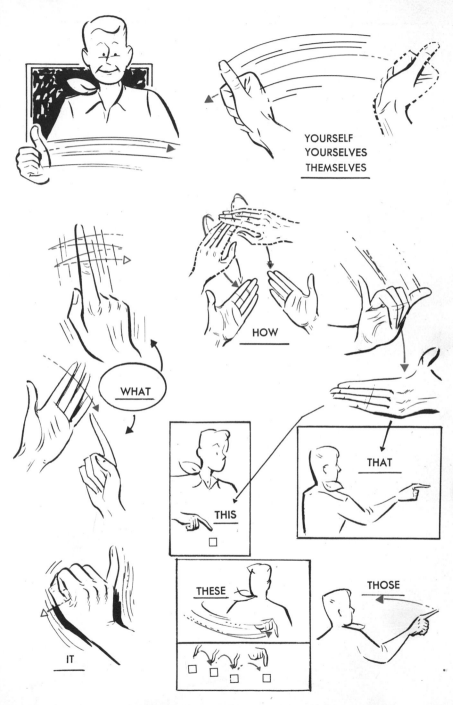

YOURSELF
YOURSELVES
THEMSELVES

HOW

WHAT

THAT

THIS

THESE

THOSE

IT

3

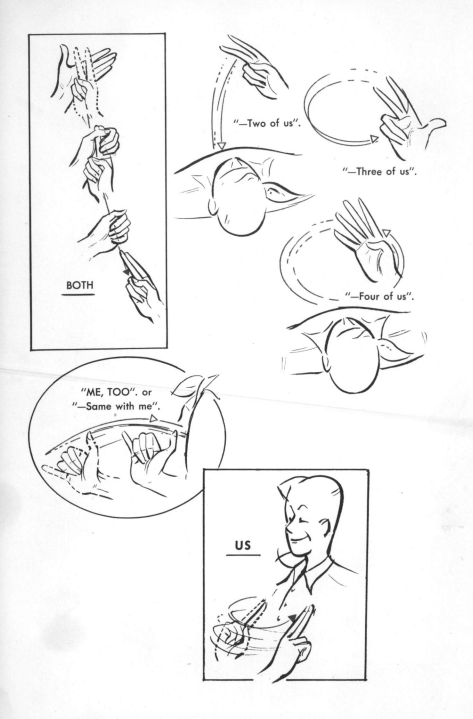

"—Two of us".

"—Three of us".

"—Four of us".

BOTH

"ME, TOO". or
"—Same with me".

US

4

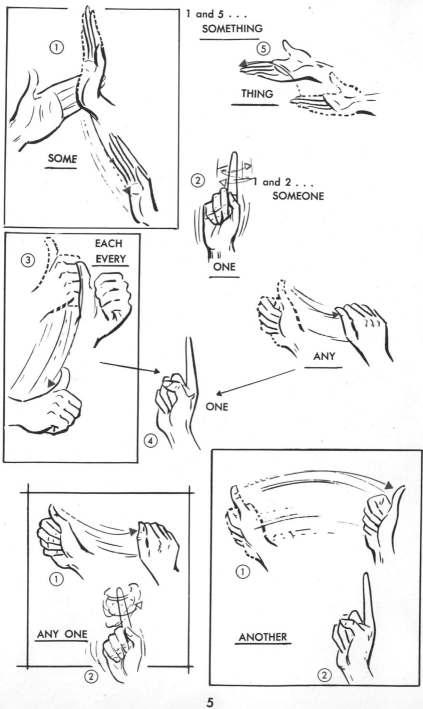

SOME

1 and 5 . . .
SOMETHING

THING

EACH
EVERY

② 1 and 2 . . .
SOMEONE

ONE

ANY

ONE

④

ANY ONE

ANOTHER

5

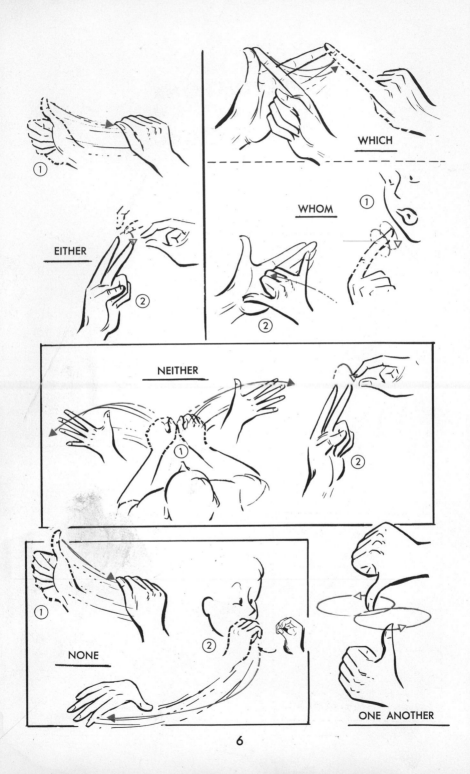

WHICH

WHOM

EITHER

NEITHER

NONE

ONE ANOTHER

6

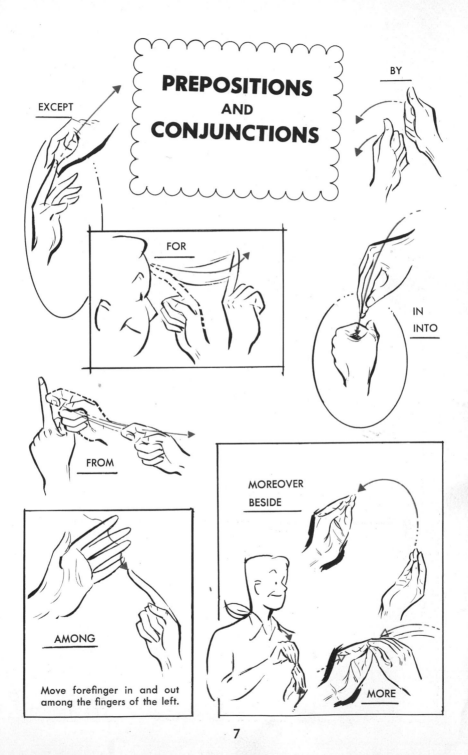

EXCEPT

PREPOSITIONS
AND
CONJUNCTIONS

BY

FOR

IN
INTO

FROM

MOREOVER
BESIDE

AMONG

Move forefinger in and out among the fingers of the left.

MORE

7

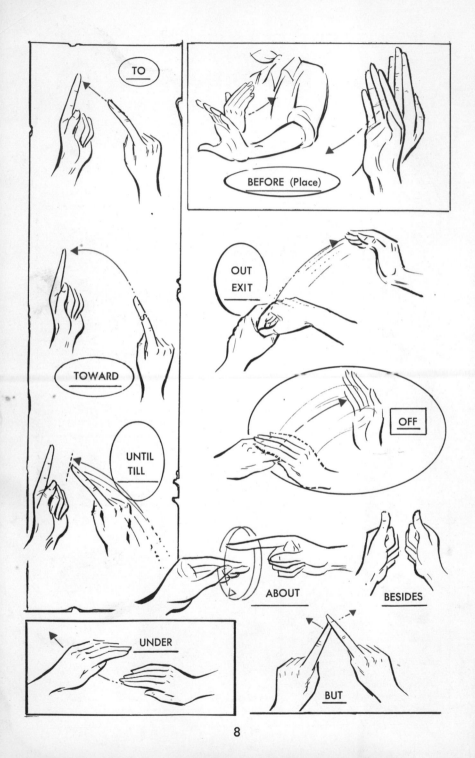

TO

BEFORE (Place)

OUT
EXIT

TOWARD

OFF

UNTIL
TILL

ABOUT

BESIDES

UNDER

BUT

8

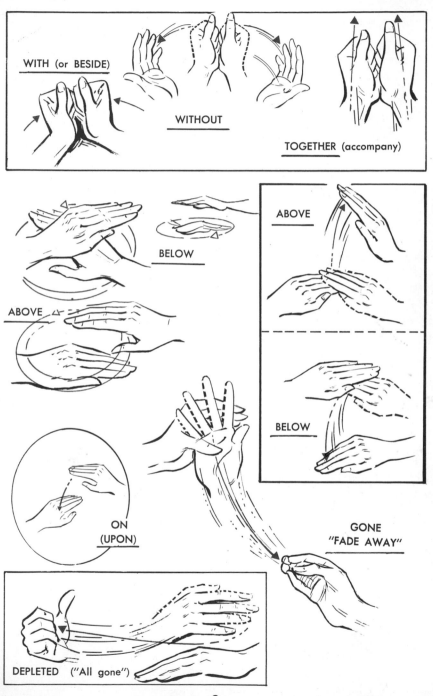

WITH (or BESIDE)

WITHOUT

TOGETHER (accompany)

BELOW

ABOVE

ABOVE

BELOW

ON (UPON)

GONE "FADE AWAY"

DEPLETED ("All gone")

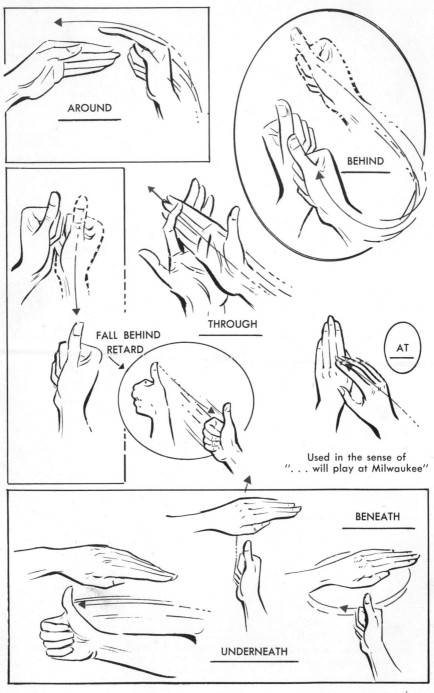

AROUND

BEHIND

THROUGH

FALL BEHIND
RETARD

AT

Used in the sense of
". . . will play at Milwaukee"

BENEATH

UNDERNEATH

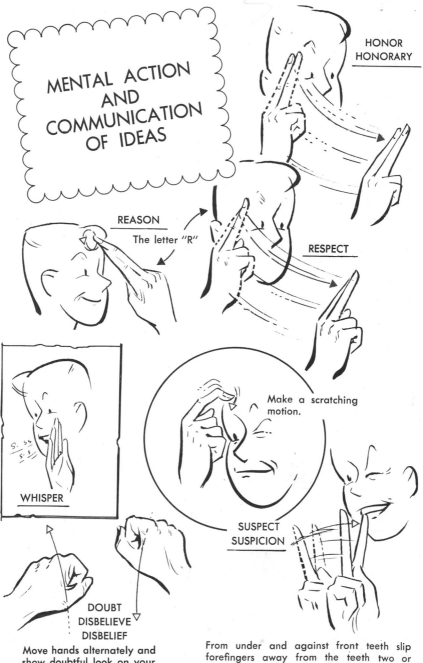

MENTAL ACTION
AND
COMMUNICATION
OF IDEAS

HONOR
HONORARY

REASON
The letter "R"

RESPECT

WHISPER

Make a scratching motion.

SUSPECT
SUSPICION

DOUBT
DISBELIEVE
DISBELIEF

Move hands alternately and show doubtful look on your face.

From under and against front teeth slip forefingers away from the teeth two or three times.

11

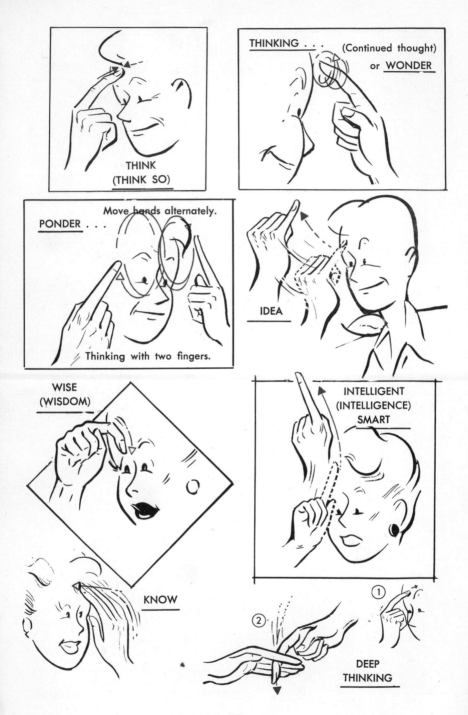

THINK
(THINK SO)

THINKING . . .   (Continued thought)
or WONDER

PONDER . . .   Move hands alternately.

Thinking with two fingers.

IDEA

WISE
(WISDOM)

INTELLIGENT
(INTELLIGENCE)
SMART

KNOW

① ②

DEEP
THINKING

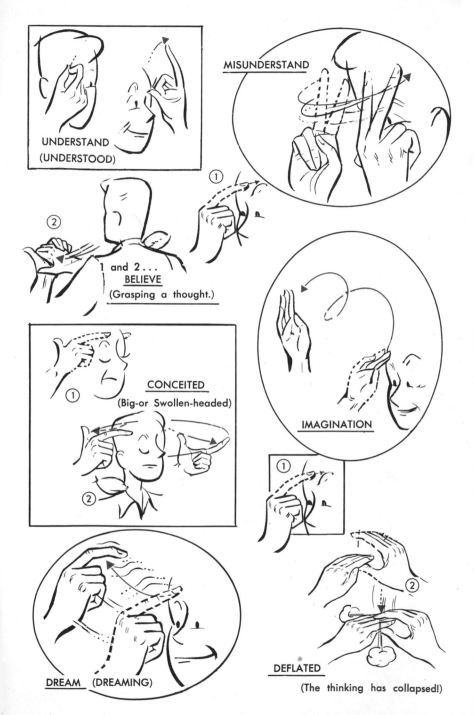

UNDERSTAND
(UNDERSTOOD)

MISUNDERSTAND

① ②

1 and 2 . . .
BELIEVE
(Grasping a thought.)

CONCEITED
(Big- or Swollen-headed)
①
②

IMAGINATION

DREAM (DREAMING)

①
②
DEFLATED
(The thinking has collapsed!)

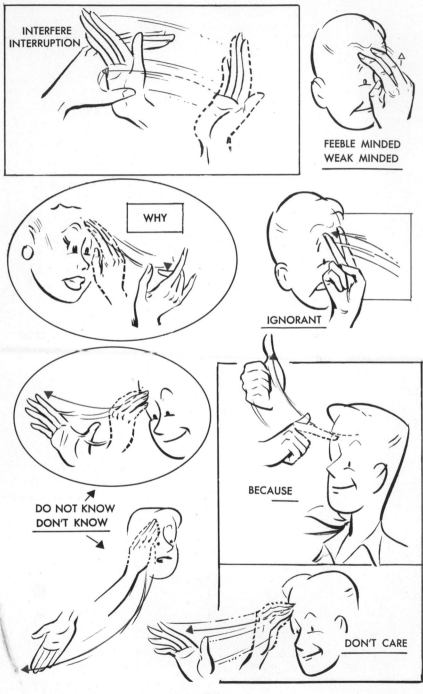

INTERFERE
INTERRUPTION

FEEBLE MINDED
WEAK MINDED

WHY

IGNORANT

DO NOT KNOW
DON'T KNOW

BECAUSE

DON'T CARE

14

LIKE

As if the heart is being drawn out toward the object. The sign for "please" is also used to mean "like."

FASCINATE

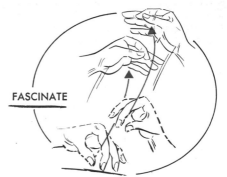

Draw away slowly from the heart giving the face an intent or concentrated look.

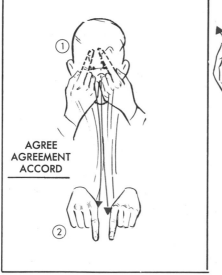

AGREE AGREEMENT ACCORD

INFORM NOTIFY

INTEND MEAN PURPOSE

SHOW DISPLAY DEMONSTRATE

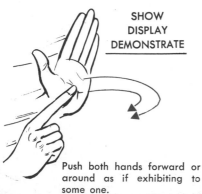

Push both hands forward or around as if exhibiting to some one.

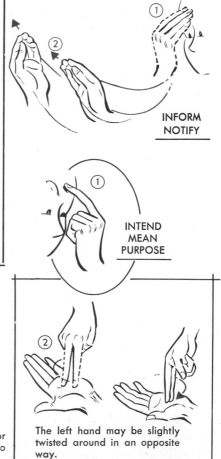

The left hand may be slightly twisted around in an opposite way.

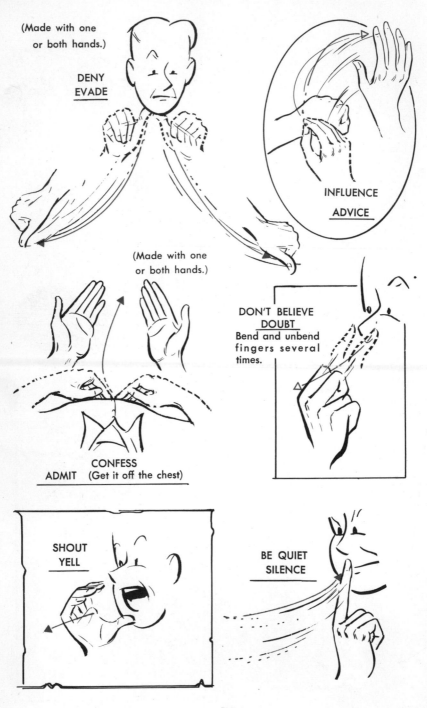

(Made with one or both hands.)

DENY
EVADE

INFLUENCE
ADVICE

(Made with one or both hands.)

DON'T BELIEVE
DOUBT
Bend and unbend fingers several times.

CONFESS
ADMIT   (Get it off the chest)

SHOUT
YELL

BE QUIET
SILENCE

16

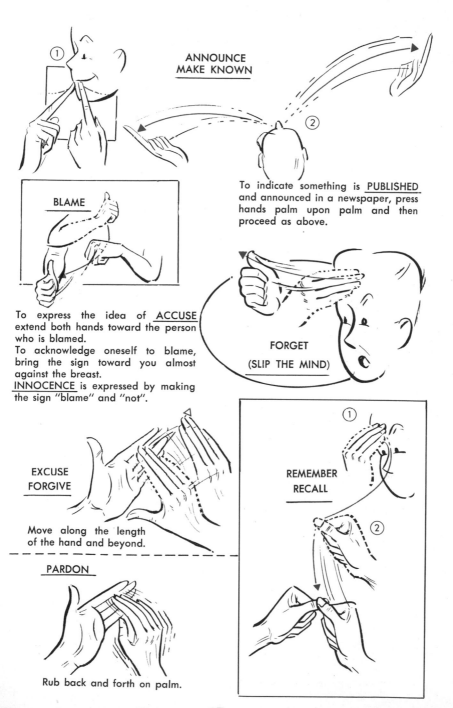

ANNOUNCE
MAKE KNOWN

BLAME

To indicate something is PUBLISHED and announced in a newspaper, press hands palm upon palm and then proceed as above.

To express the idea of ACCUSE extend both hands toward the person who is blamed.
To acknowledge oneself to blame, bring the sign toward you almost against the breast.
INNOCENCE is expressed by making the sign "blame" and "not".

FORGET
(SLIP THE MIND)

EXCUSE
FORGIVE

Move along the length of the hand and beyond.

REMEMBER
RECALL

PARDON

Rub back and forth on palm.

17

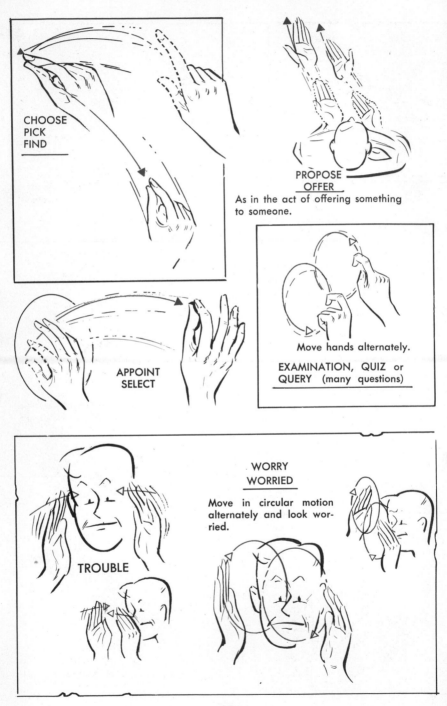

CHOOSE
PICK
FIND

PROPOSE
OFFER
As in the act of offering something
to someone.

APPOINT
SELECT

Move hands alternately.

EXAMINATION, QUIZ or
QUERY (many questions)

WORRY
WORRIED

Move in circular motion
alternately and look wor-
ried.

TROUBLE

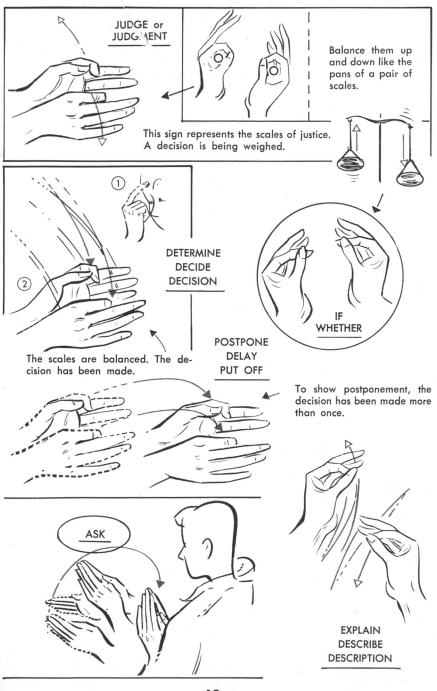

JUDGE or JUDGMENT

This sign represents the scales of justice. A decision is being weighed.

Balance them up and down like the pans of a pair of scales.

DETERMINE
DECIDE
DECISION

IF
WHETHER

The scales are balanced. The decision has been made.

POSTPONE
DELAY
PUT OFF

To show postponement, the decision has been made more than once.

ASK

EXPLAIN
DESCRIBE
DESCRIPTION

19

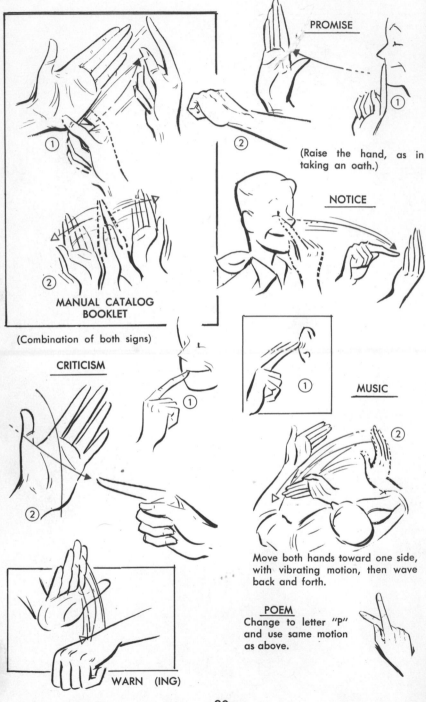

PROMISE

(Raise the hand, as in taking an oath.)

MANUAL CATALOG BOOKLET

(Combination of both signs)

NOTICE

CRITICISM

MUSIC

Move both hands toward one side, with vibrating motion, then wave back and forth.

POEM
Change to letter "P" and use same motion as above.

WARN (ING)

20

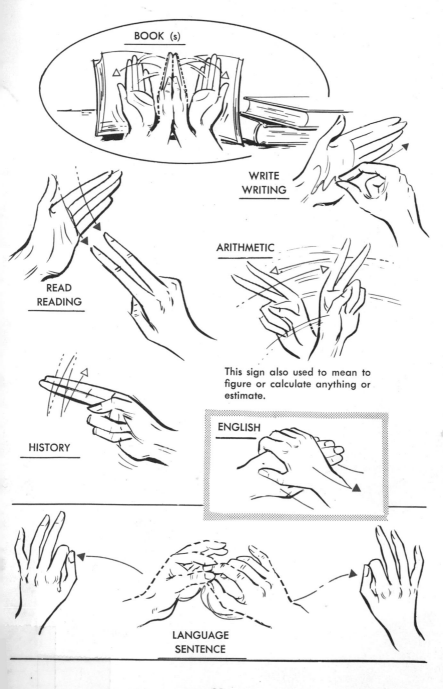

BOOK (s)

WRITE
WRITING

READ
READING

ARITHMETIC

HISTORY

This sign also used to mean to figure or calculate anything or estimate.

ENGLISH

LANGUAGE
SENTENCE

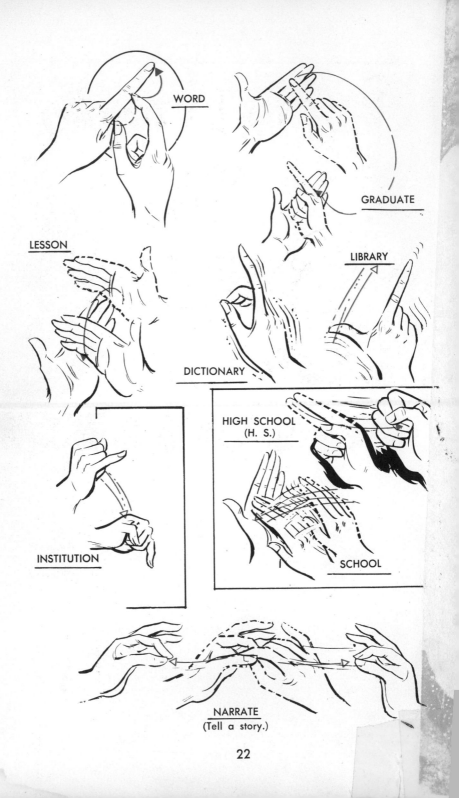

WORD

GRADUATE

LESSON

LIBRARY

DICTIONARY

HIGH SCHOOL
(H. S.)

INSTITUTION

SCHOOL

NARRATE
(Tell a story.)

22

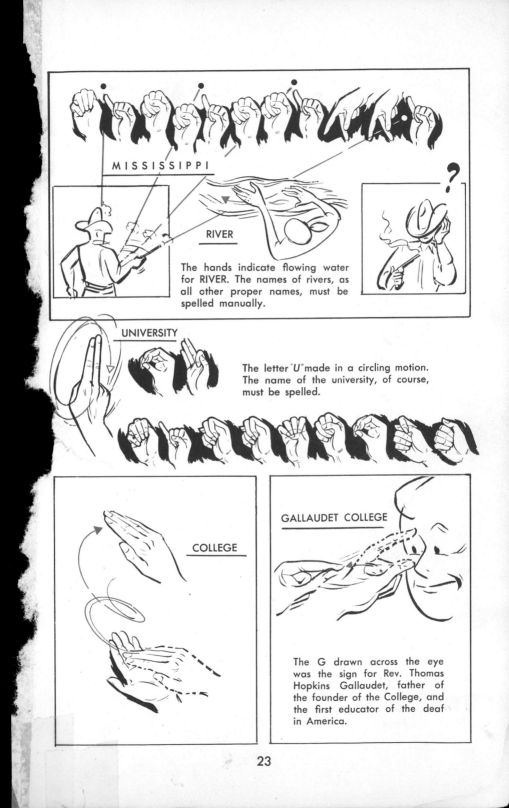

MISSISSIPPI

RIVER

The hands indicate flowing water for RIVER. The names of rivers, as all other proper names, must be spelled manually.

UNIVERSITY

The letter "U" made in a circling motion. The name of the university, of course, must be spelled.

COLLEGE

GALLAUDET COLLEGE

The G drawn across the eye was the sign for Rev. Thomas Hopkins Gallaudet, father of the founder of the College, and the first educator of the deaf in America.

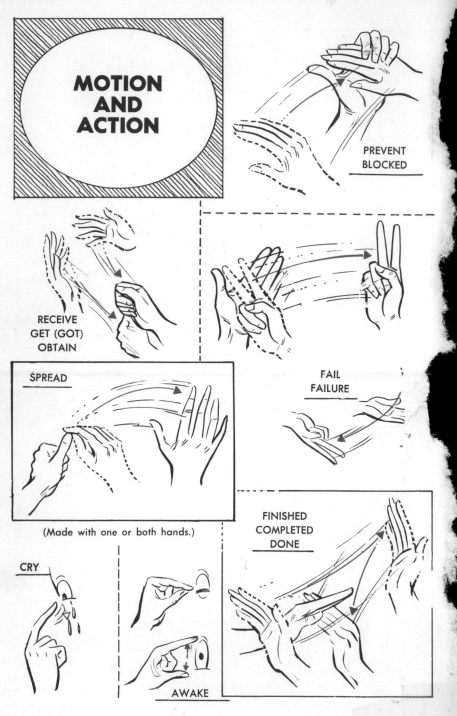

MOTION AND ACTION

PREVENT
BLOCKED

RECEIVE
GET (GOT)
OBTAIN

FAIL
FAILURE

SPREAD

(Made with one or both hands.)

FINISHED
COMPLETED
DONE

CRY

AWAKE

24

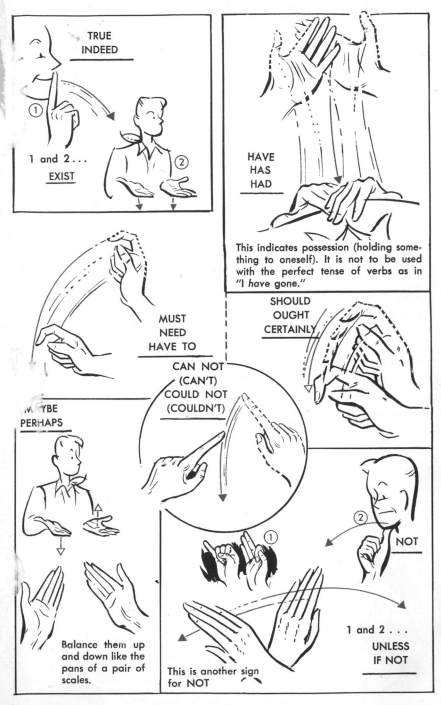

TRUE
INDEED

1 and 2...
EXIST

HAVE
HAS
HAD

This indicates possession (holding something to oneself). It is not to be used with the perfect tense of verbs as in "I *have* gone."

MUST
NEED
HAVE TO

SHOULD
OUGHT
CERTAINLY

CAN NOT
(CAN'T)
COULD NOT
(COULDN'T)

MAYBE
PERHAPS

NOT

Balance them up and down like the pans of a pair of scales.

This is another sign for NOT

1 and 2 . . .
UNLESS
IF NOT

25

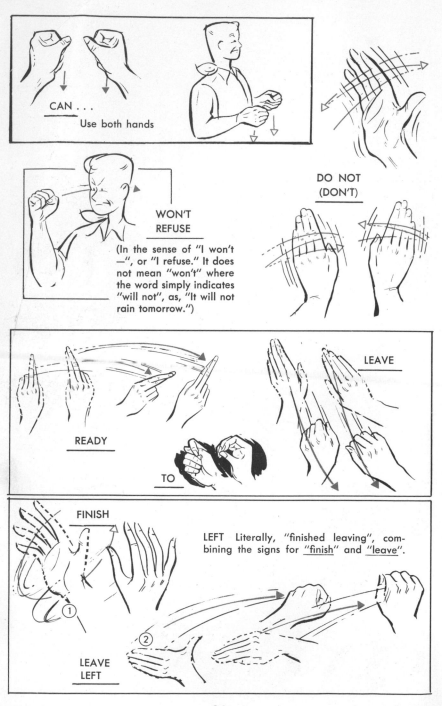

CAN . . .
Use both hands

WON'T
REFUSE

(In the sense of "I won't
—", or "I refuse." It does
not mean "won't" where
the word simply indicates
"will not", as, "It will not
rain tomorrow.")

DO NOT
(DON'T)

READY

TO

LEAVE

FINISH

LEFT Literally, "finished leaving", combining the signs for "finish" and "leave".

LEAVE
LEFT

26

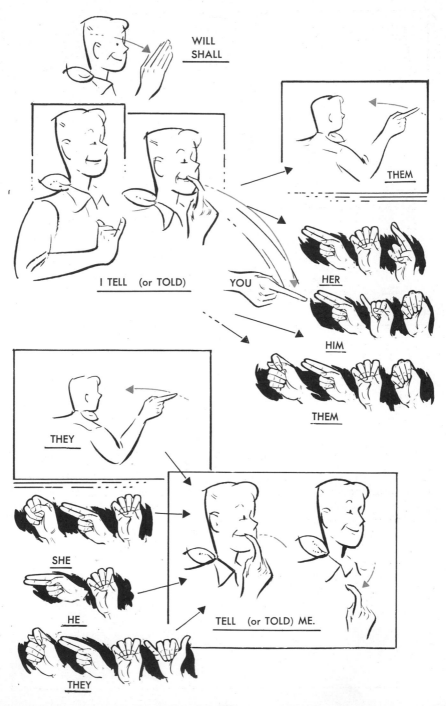

WILL
SHALL

THEM

I TELL (or TOLD)   YOU   HER

HIM

THEM

THEY

SHE

HE

TELL (or TOLD) ME.

THEY

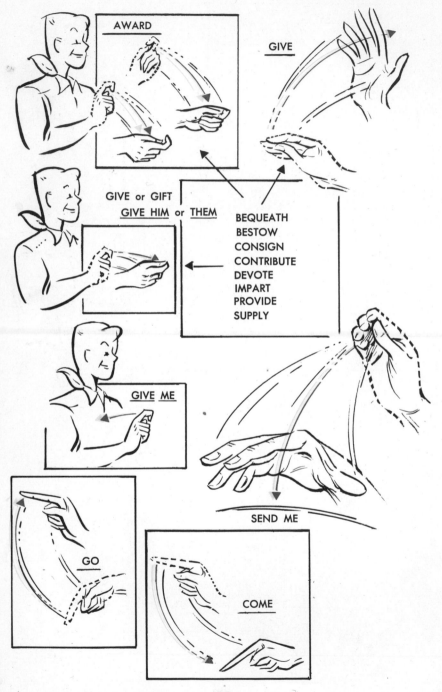

AWARD

GIVE

GIVE or GIFT
GIVE HIM or THEM

BEQUEATH
BESTOW
CONSIGN
CONTRIBUTE
DEVOTE
IMPART
PROVIDE
SUPPLY

GIVE ME

SEND ME

GO

COME

28

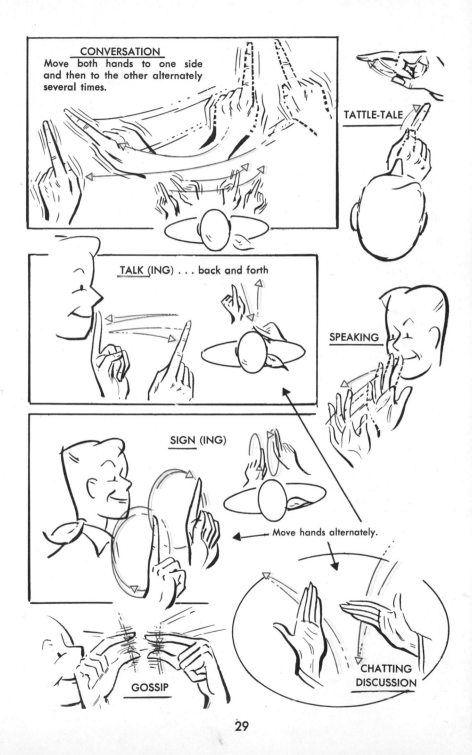

CONVERSATION
Move both hands to one side and then to the other alternately several times.

TATTLE-TALE

TALK (ING) . . . back and forth

SPEAKING

SIGN (ING)

Move hands alternately.

GOSSIP

CHATTING
DISCUSSION

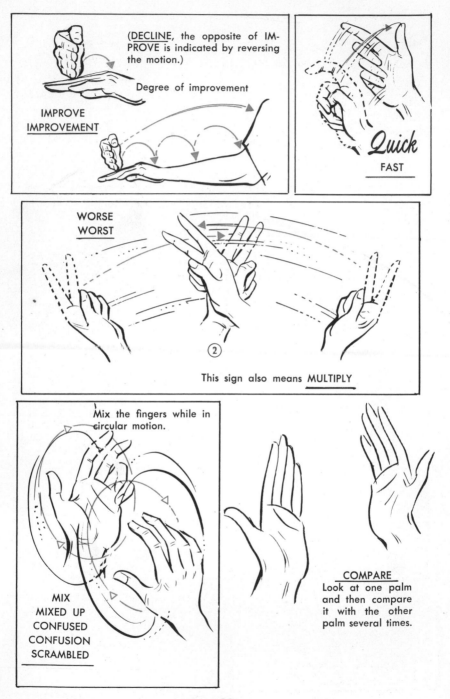

(DECLINE, the opposite of IM-PROVE is indicated by reversing the motion.)

Degree of improvement

IMPROVE
IMPROVEMENT

Quick
FAST

WORSE
WORST

②

This sign also means MULTIPLY

Mix the fingers while in circular motion.

MIX
MIXED UP
CONFUSED
CONFUSION
SCRAMBLED

COMPARE
Look at one palm and then compare it with the other palm several times.

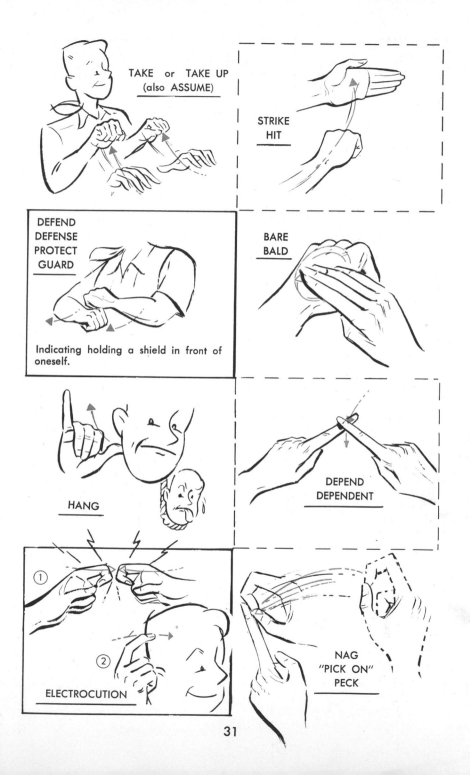

TAKE or TAKE UP
(also ASSUME)

STRIKE
HIT

DEFEND
DEFENSE
PROTECT
GUARD

Indicating holding a shield in front of oneself.

BARE
BALD

HANG

DEPEND
DEPENDENT

① ②

ELECTROCUTION

NAG
"PICK ON"
PECK

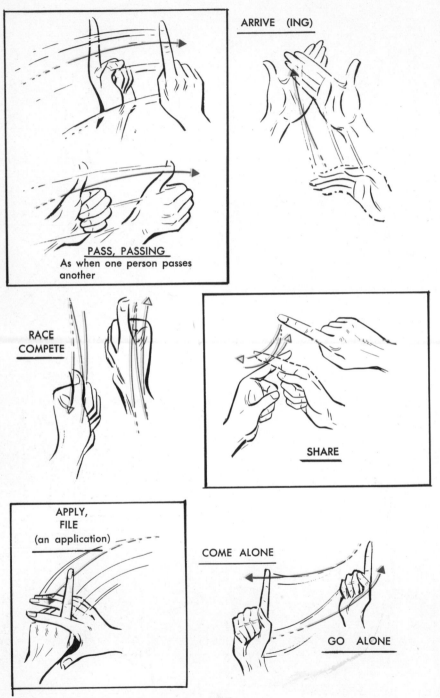

ARRIVE (ING)

PASS, PASSING
As when one person passes
another

RACE
COMPETE

SHARE

APPLY,
FILE
(an application)

COME ALONE

GO ALONE

32

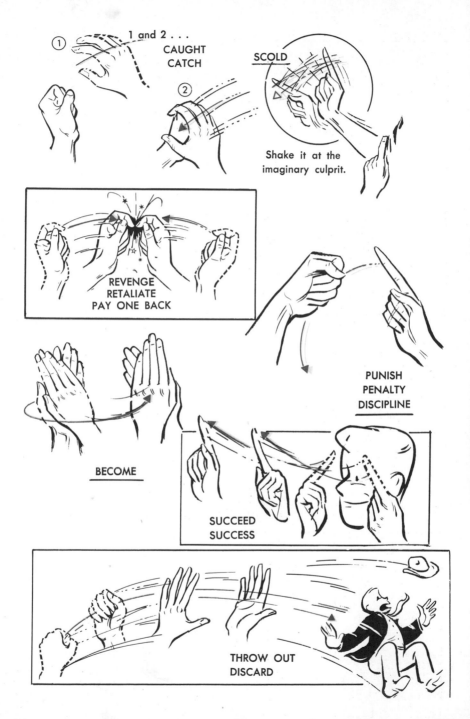

1 and 2 . . .
CAUGHT
CATCH

SCOLD

Shake it at the
imaginary culprit.

REVENGE
RETALIATE
PAY ONE BACK

PUNISH
PENALTY
DISCIPLINE

BECOME

SUCCEED
SUCCESS

THROW OUT
DISCARD

33

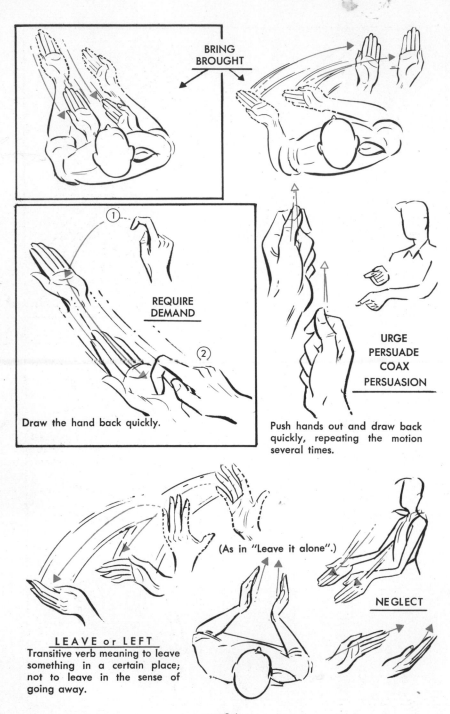

BRING
BROUGHT

REQUIRE
DEMAND

Draw the hand back quickly.

URGE
PERSUADE
COAX
PERSUASION

Push hands out and draw back quickly, repeating the motion several times.

(As in "Leave it alone".)

NEGLECT

LEAVE or LEFT
Transitive verb meaning to leave something in a certain place; not to leave in the sense of going away.

34

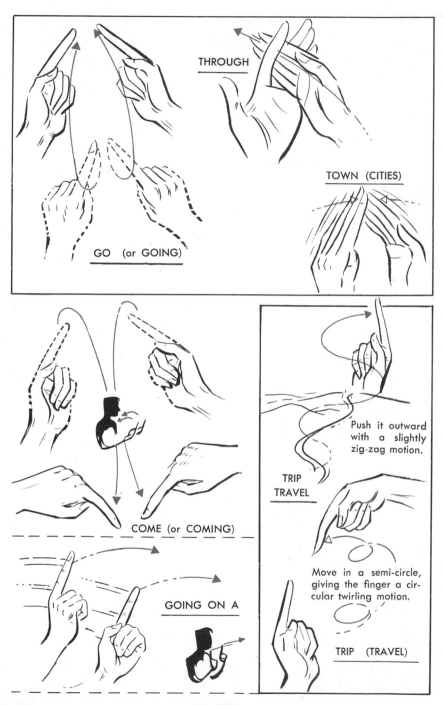

THROUGH

GO (or GOING)

TOWN (CITIES)

COME (or COMING)

GOING ON A

TRIP
TRAVEL

Push it outward with a slightly zig-zag motion.

Move in a semi-circle, giving the finger a circular twirling motion.

TRIP (TRAVEL)

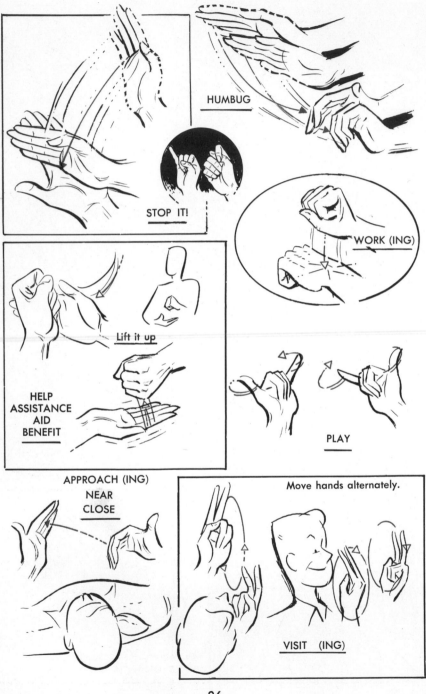

HUMBUG

STOP IT!

WORK (ING)

Lift it up

HELP
ASSISTANCE
AID
BENEFIT

PLAY

APPROACH (ING)
NEAR
CLOSE

Move hands alternately.

VISIT (ING)

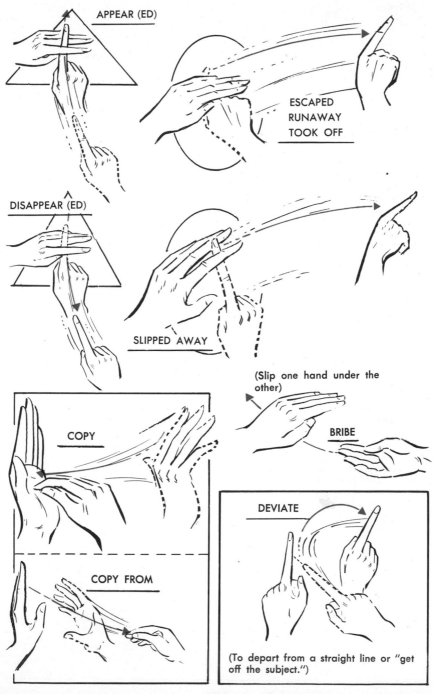

APPEAR (ED)

ESCAPED
RUNAWAY
TOOK OFF

DISAPPEAR (ED)

SLIPPED AWAY

(Slip one hand under the
other)

COPY

BRIBE

COPY FROM

DEVIATE

(To depart from a straight line or "get
off the subject.")

37

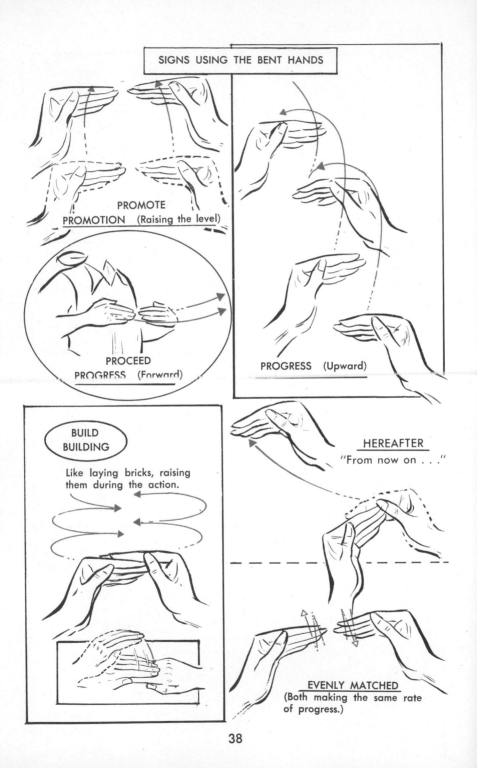

SIGNS USING THE BENT HANDS

PROMOTE
PROMOTION (Raising the level)

PROCEED
PROGRESS (Forward)

PROGRESS (Upward)

BUILD
BUILDING

Like laying bricks, raising
them during the action.

HEREAFTER
"From now on . . ."

EVENLY MATCHED
(Both making the same rate
of progress.)

38

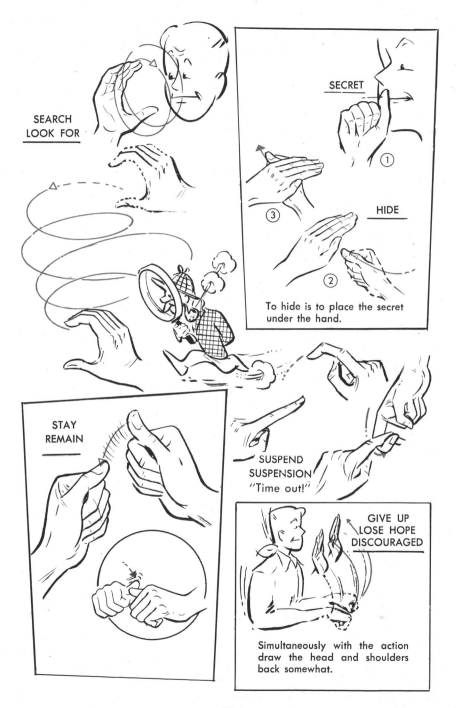

SEARCH
LOOK FOR

SECRET

HIDE

①

②

③

To hide is to place the secret under the hand.

STAY
REMAIN

SUSPEND
SUSPENSION
"Time out!"

GIVE UP
LOSE HOPE
DISCOURAGED

Simultaneously with the action draw the head and shoulders back somewhat.

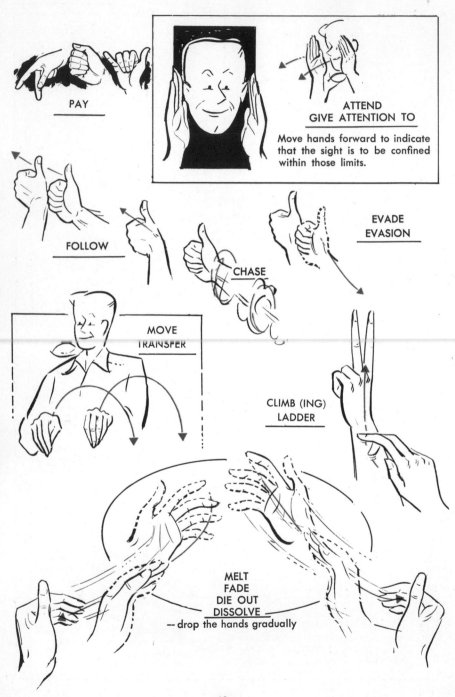

PAY

ATTEND
GIVE ATTENTION TO

Move hands forward to indicate that the sight is to be confined within those limits.

FOLLOW

CHASE

EVADE
EVASION

MOVE
TRANSFER

CLIMB (ING)
LADDER

MELT
FADE
DIE OUT
DISSOLVE
— drop the hands gradually

40

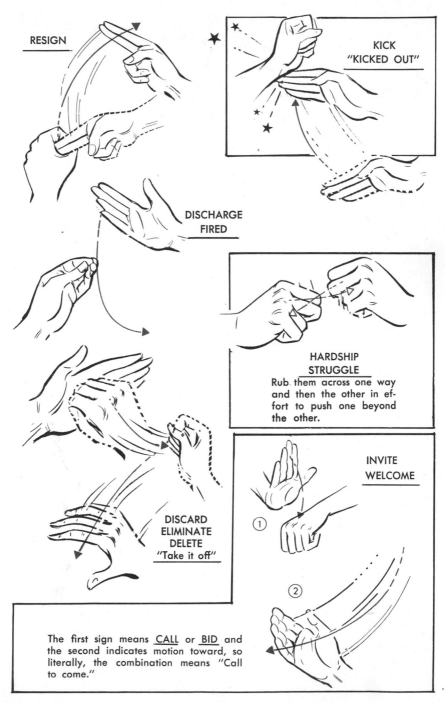

RESIGN

KICK
"KICKED OUT"

DISCHARGE
FIRED

HARDSHIP
STRUGGLE
Rub them across one way
and then the other in ef-
fort to push one beyond
the other.

INVITE
WELCOME

①

②

DISCARD
ELIMINATE
DELETE
"Take it off"

The first sign means <u>CALL</u> or <u>BID</u> and
the second indicates motion toward, so
literally, the combination means "Call
to come."

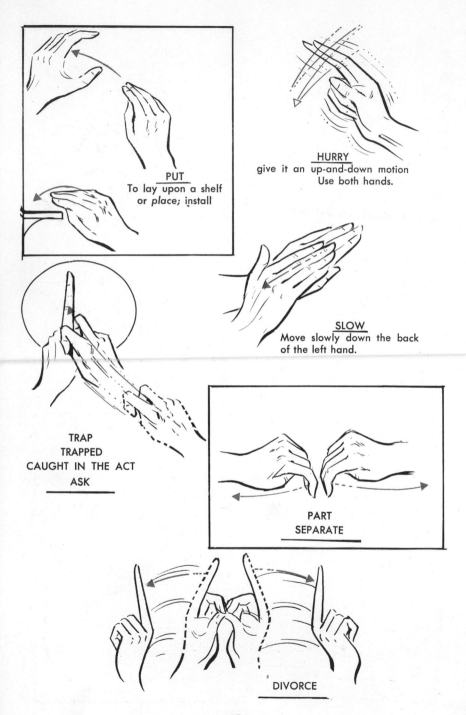

PUT
To lay upon a shelf
or *place*; install

HURRY
give it an up-and-down motion
Use both hands.

SLOW
Move slowly down the back
of the left hand.

TRAP
TRAPPED
CAUGHT IN THE ACT
ASK

PART
SEPARATE

DIVORCE

42

SENSATIONS
FEELINGS
AND
AFFECTIONS

LOVE
Press over the heart

LAUGH
SMILE ①

1 and 2 . . .
CHEERFUL

② Move fingers rapidly to
indicate the "beams of
joy" radiating from the
face and look as cheerful
as you can.

HYSTERICAL LAUGH

(Rolling all over the aisle)

CONSCIENCE

THUMP!

THUMP!

JEALOUS
ENVY

43

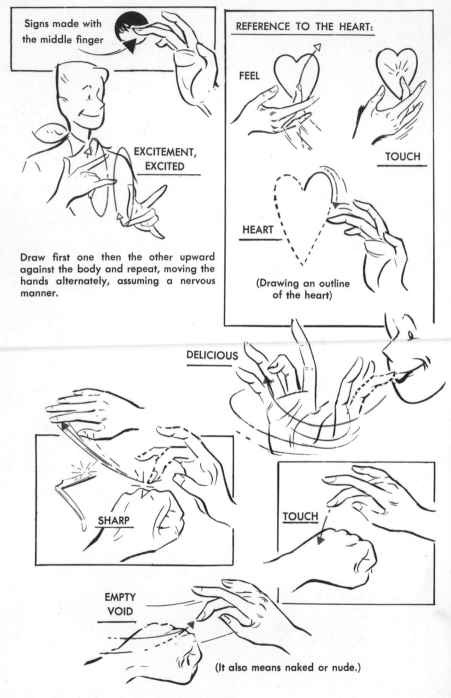

Signs made with the middle finger

EXCITEMENT, EXCITED

Draw first one then the other upward against the body and repeat, moving the hands alternately, assuming a nervous manner.

REFERENCE TO THE HEART:

FEEL

TOUCH

HEART

(Drawing an outline of the heart)

DELICIOUS

SHARP

TOUCH

EMPTY VOID

(It also means naked or nude.)

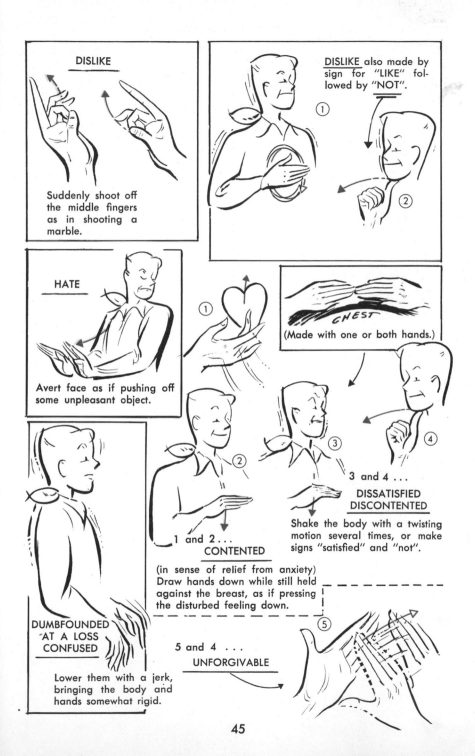

DISLIKE

Suddenly shoot off the middle fingers as in shooting a marble.

DISLIKE also made by sign for "LIKE" followed by "NOT".

① ②

HATE

Avert face as if pushing off some unpleasant object.

①

②

③

④

CHEST

(Made with one or both hands.)

1 and 2 . . .
CONTENTED

(in sense of relief from anxiety) Draw hands down while still held against the breast, as if pressing the disturbed feeling down.

3 and 4 . . .
DISSATISFIED
DISCONTENTED

Shake the body with a twisting motion several times, or make signs "satisfied" and "not".

DUMBFOUNDED
AT A LOSS
CONFUSED

Lower them with a jerk, bringing the body and hands somewhat rigid.

5 and 4 . . .
UNFORGIVABLE

⑤

45

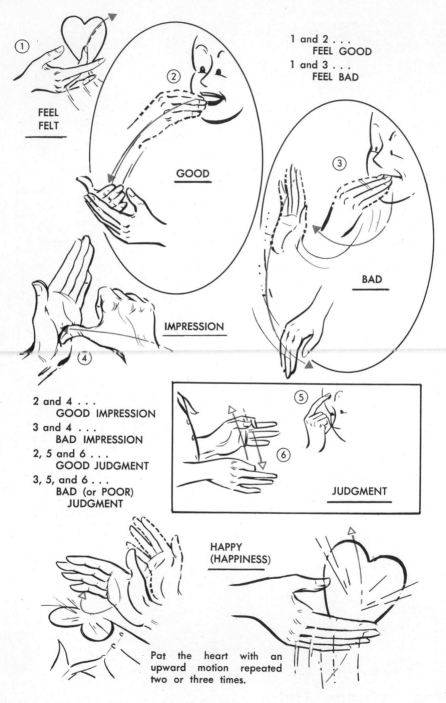

① FEEL
FELT

1 and 2 . . .
   FEEL GOOD
1 and 3 . . .
   FEEL BAD

② GOOD

③ BAD

④ IMPRESSION

2 and 4 . . .
   GOOD IMPRESSION
3 and 4 . . .
   BAD IMPRESSION
2, 5 and 6 . . .
   GOOD JUDGMENT
3, 5, and 6 . . .
   BAD (or POOR)
   JUDGMENT

⑤ ⑥ JUDGMENT

HAPPY
(HAPPINESS)

Pat the heart with an
upward motion repeated
two or three times.

46

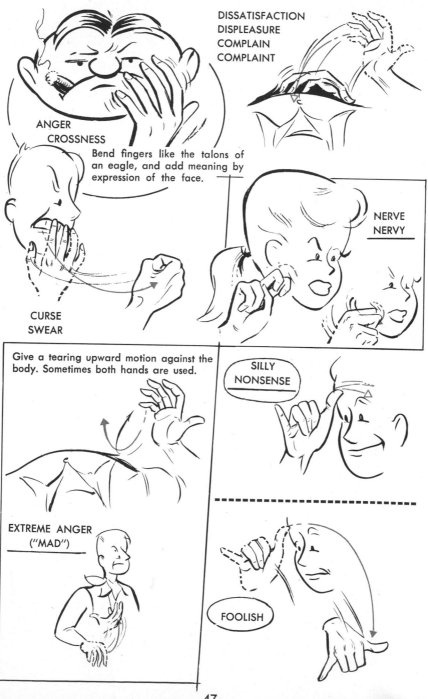

DISSATISFACTION
DISPLEASURE
COMPLAIN
COMPLAINT

ANGER
CROSSNESS

Bend fingers like the talons of an eagle, and add meaning by expression of the face.

CURSE
SWEAR

NERVE
NERVY

Give a tearing upward motion against the body. Sometimes both hands are used.

SILLY
NONSENSE

EXTREME ANGER
("MAD")

FOOLISH

47

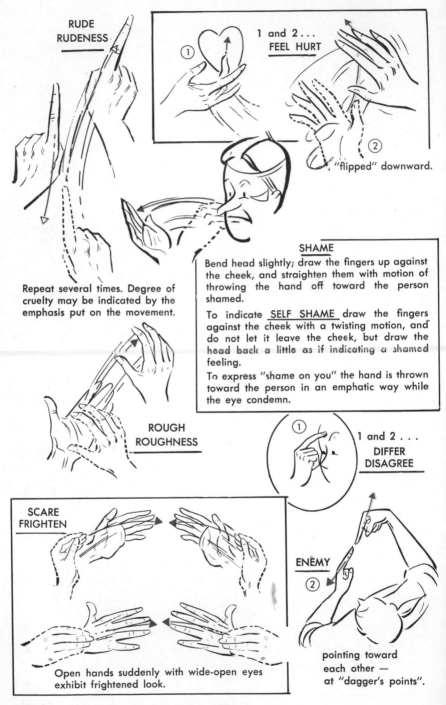

RUDE
RUDENESS

1 and 2 . . .
FEEL HURT

① ②

"flipped" downward.

Repeat several times. Degree of cruelty may be indicated by the emphasis put on the movement.

SHAME

Bend head slightly; draw the fingers up against the cheek, and straighten them with motion of throwing the hand off toward the person shamed.

To indicate SELF SHAME draw the fingers against the cheek with a twisting motion, and do not let it leave the cheek, but draw the head back a little as if indicating a shamed feeling.

To express "shame on you" the hand is thrown toward the person in an emphatic way while the eye condemn.

ROUGH
ROUGHNESS

① 1 and 2 . . .
DIFFER
DISAGREE

SCARE
FRIGHTEN

ENEMY
②

Open hands suddenly with wide-open eyes exhibit frightened look.

pointing toward each other — at "dagger's points".

48

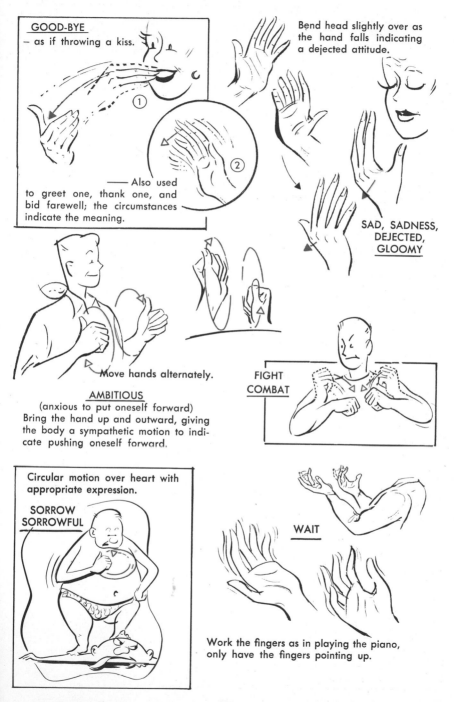

GOOD-BYE
— as if throwing a kiss.

① ②

———— Also used to greet one, thank one, and bid farewell; the circumstances indicate the meaning.

Bend head slightly over as the hand falls indicating a dejected attitude.

SAD, SADNESS, DEJECTED, GLOOMY

Move hands alternately.

AMBITIOUS
(anxious to put oneself forward)
Bring the hand up and outward, giving the body a sympathetic motion to indicate pushing oneself forward.

FIGHT COMBAT

Circular motion over heart with appropriate expression.

SORROW SORROWFUL

WAIT

Work the fingers as in playing the piano, only have the fingers pointing up.

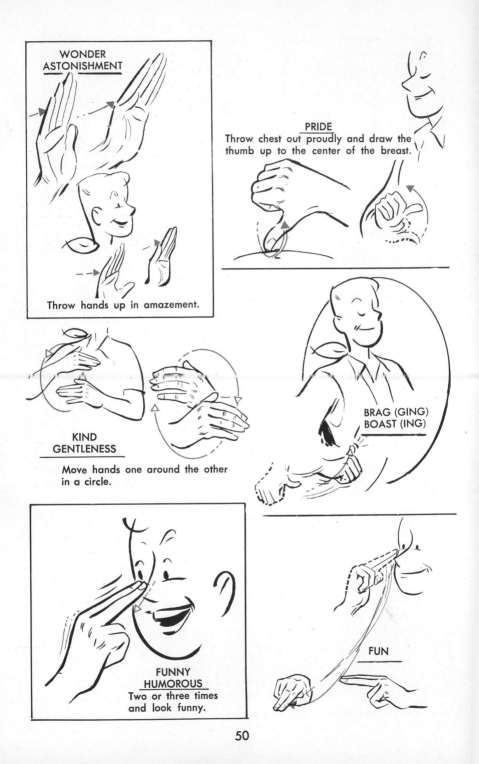

WONDER
ASTONISHMENT

Throw hands up in amazement.

PRIDE
Throw chest out proudly and draw the
thumb up to the center of the breast.

KIND
GENTLENESS

Move hands one around the other
in a circle.

BRAG (GING)
BOAST (ING)

FUNNY
HUMOROUS
Two or three times
and look funny.

FUN

50

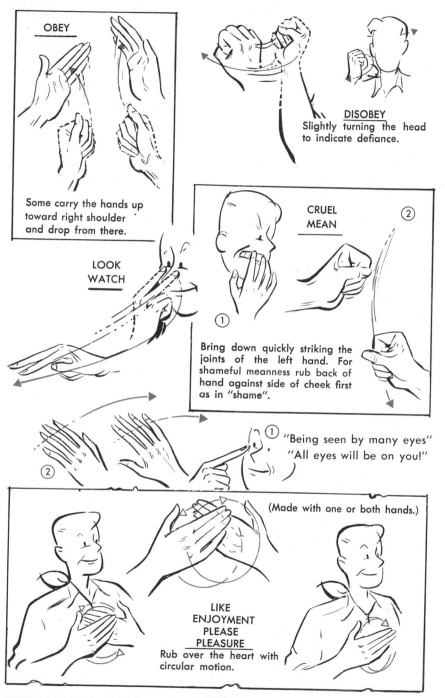

OBEY

Some carry the hands up toward right shoulder and drop from there.

DISOBEY
Slightly turning the head to indicate defiance.

LOOK WATCH

CRUEL MEAN

②

① Bring down quickly striking the joints of the left hand. For shameful meanness rub back of hand against side of cheek first as in "shame".

① "Being seen by many eyes"
"All eyes will be on you!"

②

(Made with one or both hands.)

**LIKE
ENJOYMENT
PLEASE
PLEASURE**
Rub over the heart with circular motion.

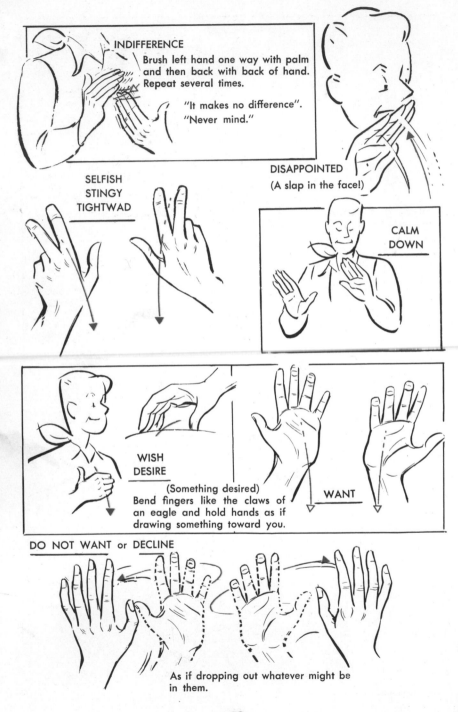

INDIFFERENCE

Brush left hand one way with palm and then back with back of hand. Repeat several times.

"It makes no difference".
"Never mind."

**SELFISH
STINGY
TIGHTWAD**

DISAPPOINTED
(A slap in the face!)

**CALM
DOWN**

**WISH
DESIRE**

(Something desired)
Bend fingers like the claws of an eagle and hold hands as if drawing something toward you.

WANT

DO NOT WANT or DECLINE

As if dropping out whatever might be in them.

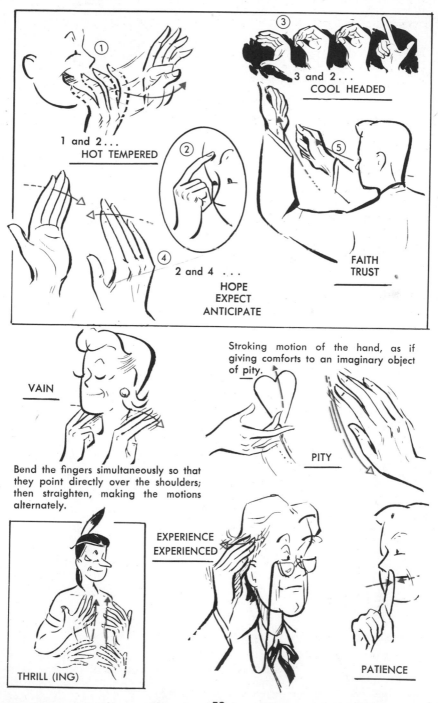

1 and 2 . . .
HOT TEMPERED

3 and 2 . . .
COOL HEADED

2 and 4 . . .
HOPE
EXPECT
ANTICIPATE

FAITH
TRUST

VAIN

Bend the fingers simultaneously so that they point directly over the shoulders; then straighten, making the motions alternately.

Stroking motion of the hand, as if giving comforts to an imaginary object of pity.

PITY

THRILL (ING)

EXPERIENCE
EXPERIENCED

PATIENCE

53

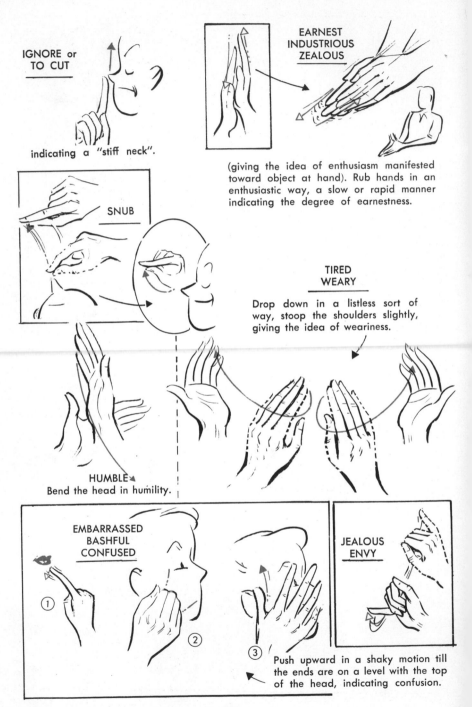

IGNORE or
TO CUT

indicating a "stiff neck".

EARNEST
INDUSTRIOUS
ZEALOUS

(giving the idea of enthusiasm manifested toward object at hand). Rub hands in an enthusiastic way, a slow or rapid manner indicating the degree of earnestness.

SNUB

TIRED
WEARY

Drop down in a listless sort of way, stoop the shoulders slightly, giving the idea of weariness.

HUMBLE
Bend the head in humility.

EMBARRASSED
BASHFUL
CONFUSED

①

②

③

JEALOUS
ENVY

Push upward in a shaky motion till the ends are on a level with the top of the head, indicating confusion.

54

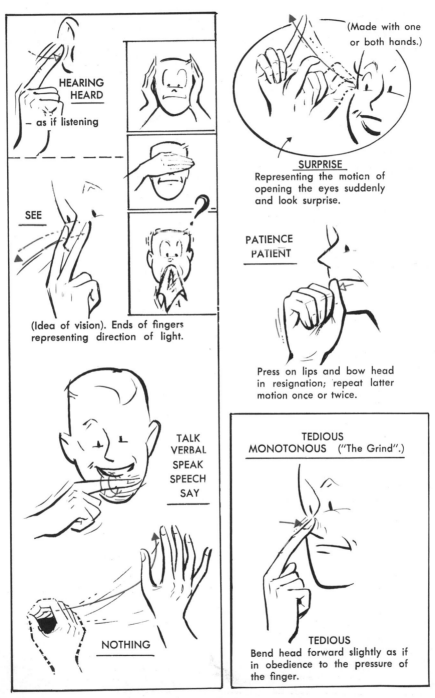

HEARING
HEARD
– as if listening

SEE

(Idea of vision). Ends of fingers representing direction of light.

(Made with one or both hands.)

SURPRISE
Representing the motion of opening the eyes suddenly and look surprise.

PATIENCE
PATIENT

Press on lips and bow head in resignation; repeat latter motion once or twice.

TALK
VERBAL
SPEAK
SPEECH
SAY

NOTHING

TEDIOUS
MONOTONOUS   ("The Grind".)

TEDIOUS
Bend head forward slightly as if in obedience to the pressure of the finger.

ADJECTIVES

ENOUGH
PLENTY

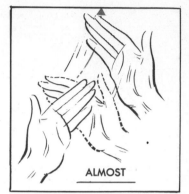

ALMOST

FRIENDLY
FRIENDSHIP
Clasp one above the other. Then bring them apart and clasp again but in opposite direction.

WILD

SMOOTH
Rub the end of the thumb against the ends of the fingers drawing the hands away from each other. The sign also indicates "of fine quality".

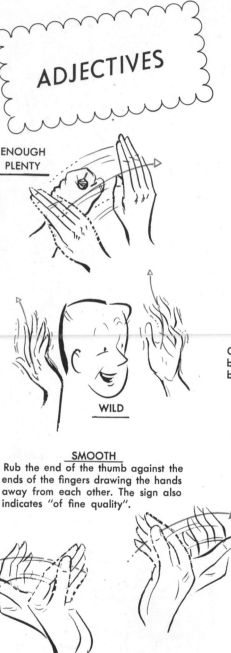

HIGH
PROMINENT

BASE
LOW

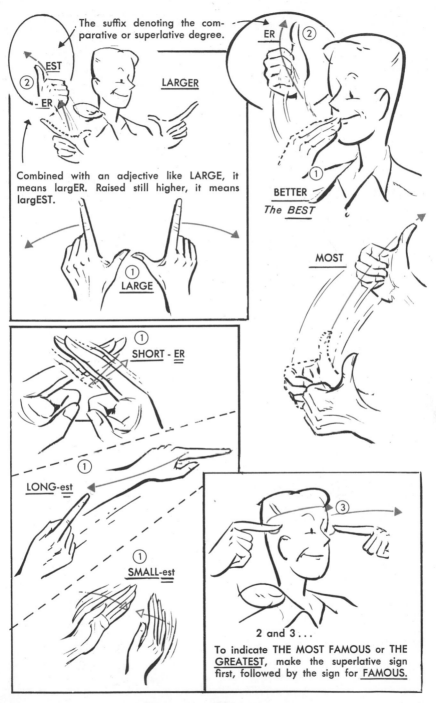

The suffix denoting the comparative or superlative degree.

EST

ER

LARGER

ER

Combined with an adjective like LARGE, it means largER. Raised still higher, it means largEST.

BETTER
The BEST

MOST

LARGE

SHORT - ER

LONG-est

SMALL-est

2 and 3 . . .
To indicate THE MOST FAMOUS or THE GREATEST, make the superlative sign first, followed by the sign for FAMOUS.

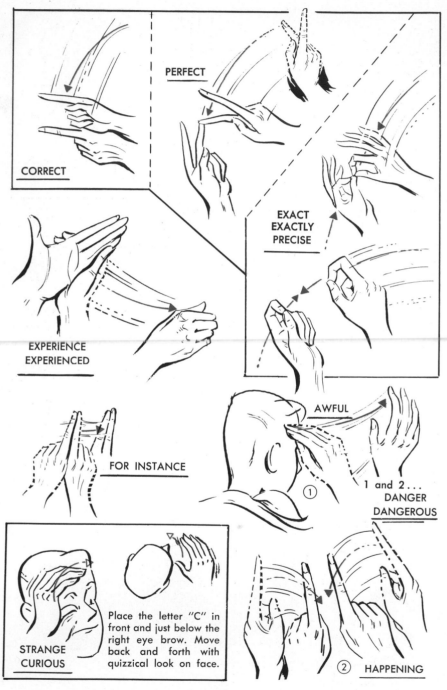

PERFECT

CORRECT

EXACT
EXACTLY
PRECISE

EXPERIENCE
EXPERIENCED

AWFUL

FOR INSTANCE

①

1 and 2...
DANGER
DANGEROUS

Place the letter "C" in front and just below the right eye brow. Move back and forth with quizzical look on face.

STRANGE
CURIOUS

② HAPPENING

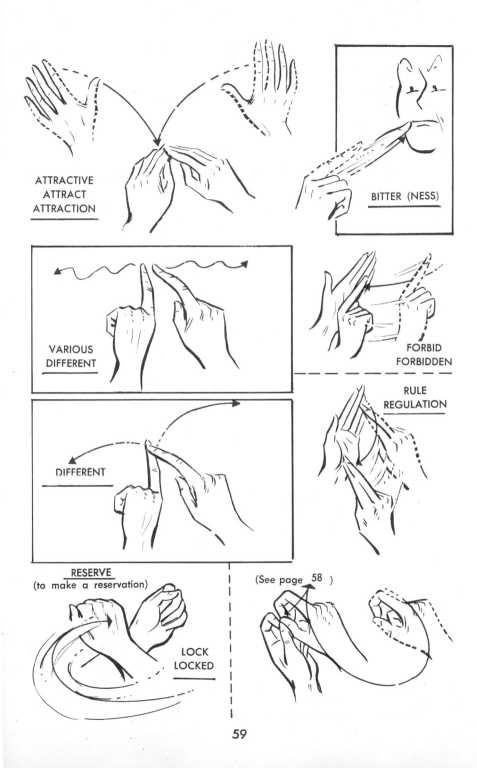

ATTRACTIVE
ATTRACT
ATTRACTION

BITTER (NESS)

VARIOUS
DIFFERENT

FORBID
FORBIDDEN

RULE
REGULATION

DIFFERENT

RESERVE
(to make a reservation)

(See page 58)

LOCK
LOCKED

59

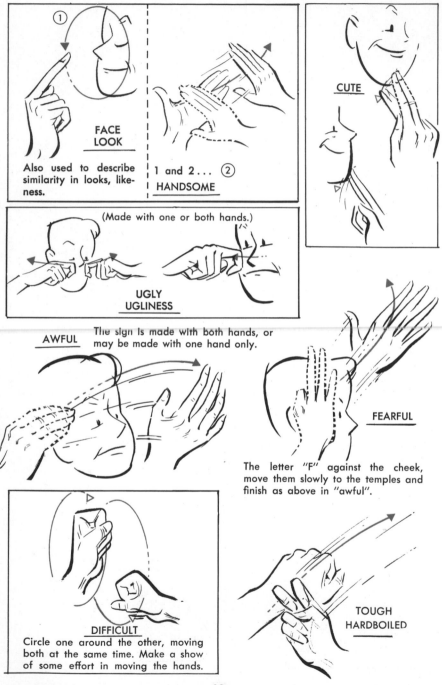

FACE
LOOK

Also used to describe similarity in looks, likeness.

1 and 2 ... ②
HANDSOME

CUTE

(Made with one or both hands.)

UGLY
UGLINESS

AWFUL

The sign is made with both hands, or may be made with one hand only.

FEARFUL

The letter "F" against the cheek, move them slowly to the temples and finish as above in "awful".

DIFFICULT

Circle one around the other, moving both at the same time. Make a show of some effort in moving the hands.

TOUGH
HARDBOILED

60

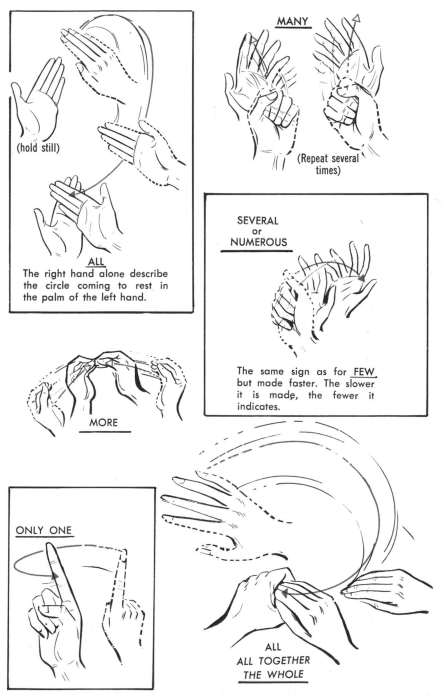

(hold still)

ALL
The right hand alone describe the circle coming to rest in the palm of the left hand.

MANY

(Repeat several times)

SEVERAL or NUMEROUS

The same sign as for **FEW** but made faster. The slower it is made, the fewer it indicates.

MORE

ONLY ONE

ALL
**ALL TOGETHER
THE WHOLE**

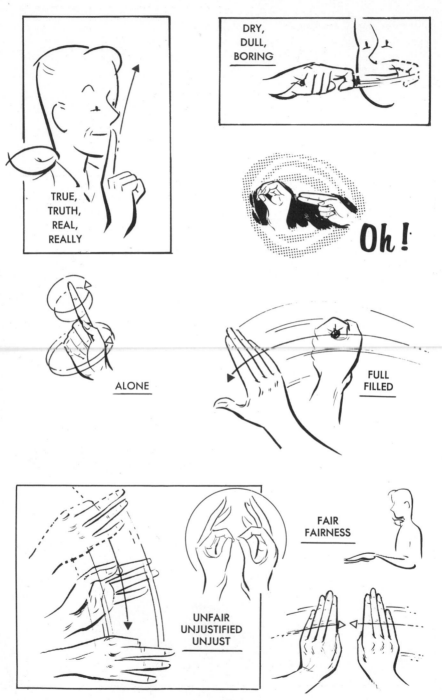

TRUE,
TRUTH,
REAL,
REALLY

DRY,
DULL,
BORING

Oh !

ALONE

FULL
FILLED

FAIR
FAIRNESS

UNFAIR
UNJUSTIFIED
UNJUST

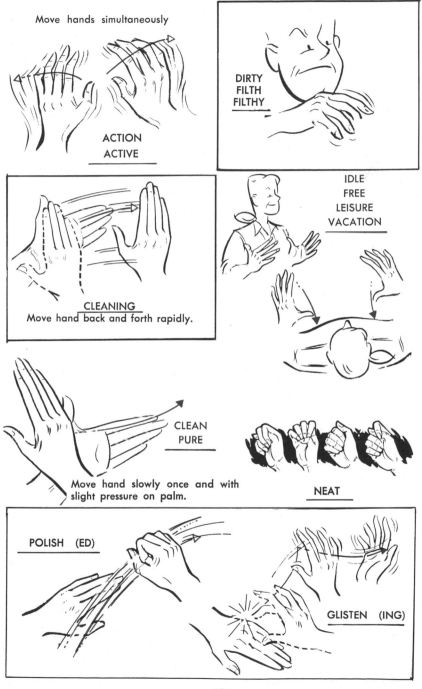

Move hands simultaneously

ACTION
ACTIVE

DIRTY
FILTH
FILTHY

CLEANING
Move hand back and forth rapidly.

IDLE
FREE
LEISURE
VACATION

CLEAN
PURE

Move hand slowly once and with
slight pressure on palm.

NEAT

POLISH (ED)

GLISTEN (ING)

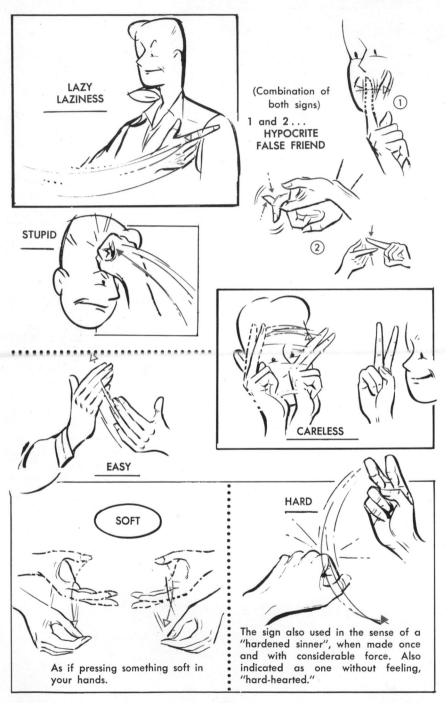

LAZY
LAZINESS

(Combination of
both signs)

1 and 2...
HYPOCRITE
FALSE FRIEND

①

②

STUPID

CARELESS

EASY

SOFT

HARD

As if pressing something soft in
your hands.

The sign also used in the sense of a
"hardened sinner", when made once
and with considerable force. Also
indicated as one without feeling,
"hard-hearted."

64

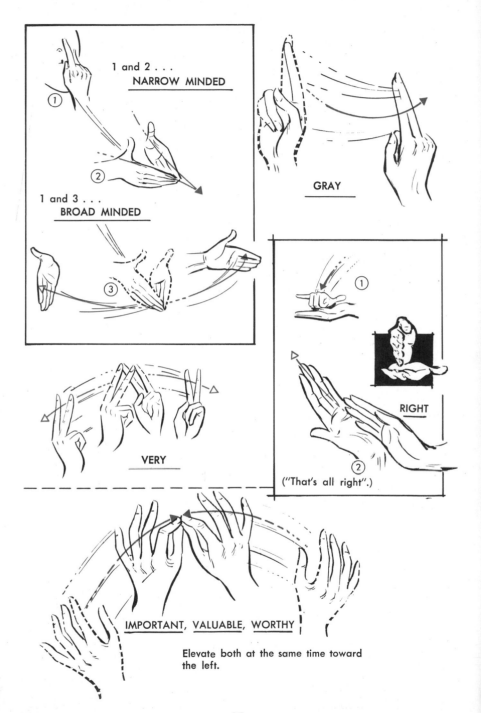

1 and 2 . . .
NARROW MINDED

1 and 3 . . .
BROAD MINDED

GRAY

VERY

RIGHT

("That's all right".)

IMPORTANT, VALUABLE, WORTHY

Elevate both at the same time toward the left.

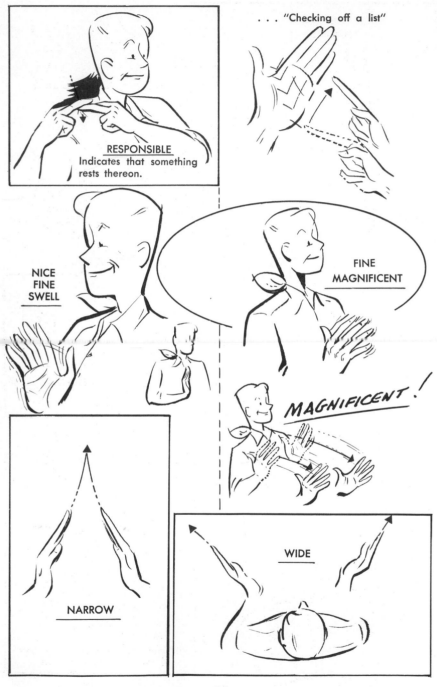

. . . "Checking off a list"

RESPONSIBLE
Indicates that something rests thereon.

NICE
FINE
SWELL

FINE
MAGNIFICENT

MAGNIFICENT!

NARROW

WIDE

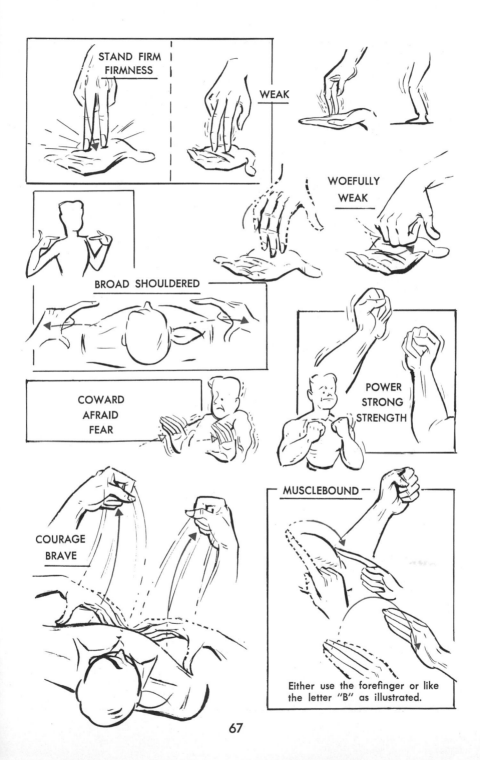

STAND FIRM
FIRMNESS

WEAK

WOEFULLY
WEAK

BROAD SHOULDERED

POWER
STRONG
STRENGTH

COWARD
AFRAID
FEAR

COURAGE
BRAVE

MUSCLEBOUND

Either use the forefinger or like
the letter "B" as illustrated.

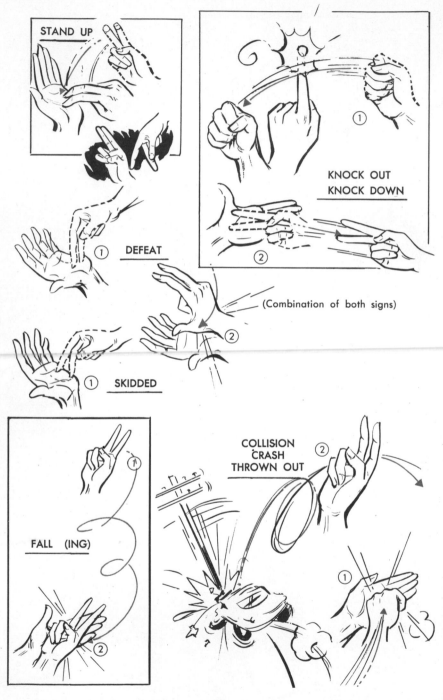

STAND UP

KNOCK OUT
KNOCK DOWN

DEFEAT

(Combination of both signs)

SKIDDED

FALL (ING)

COLLISION
CRASH
THROWN OUT

68

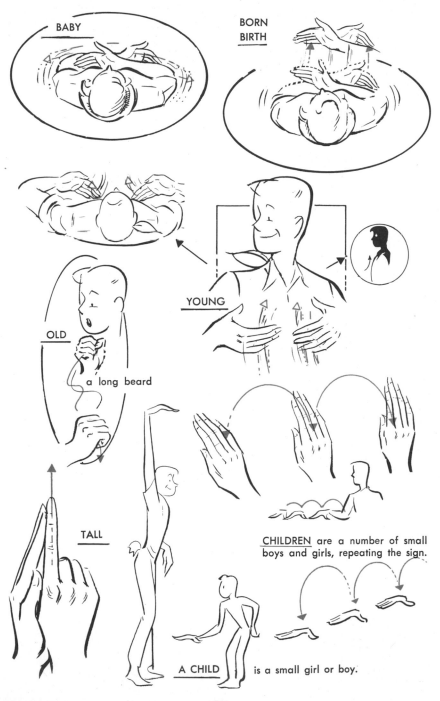

BABY

BORN BIRTH

YOUNG

OLD

a long beard

TALL

CHILDREN are a number of small boys and girls, repeating the sign.

A CHILD is a small girl or boy.

69

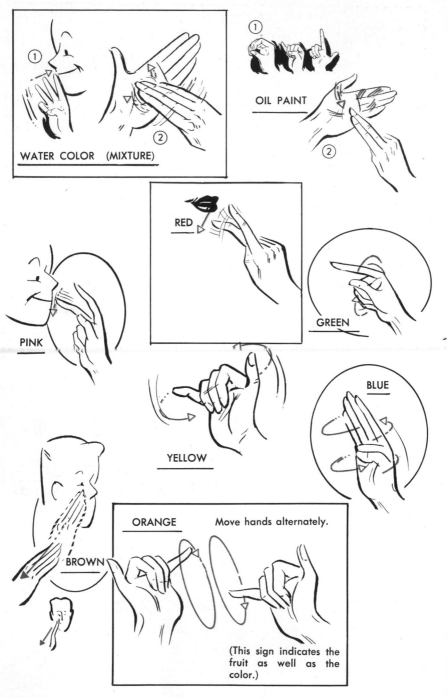

WATER COLOR (MIXTURE)

OIL PAINT

RED

GREEN

PINK

BLUE

YELLOW

BROWN

ORANGE   Move hands alternately.

(This sign indicates the fruit as well as the color.)

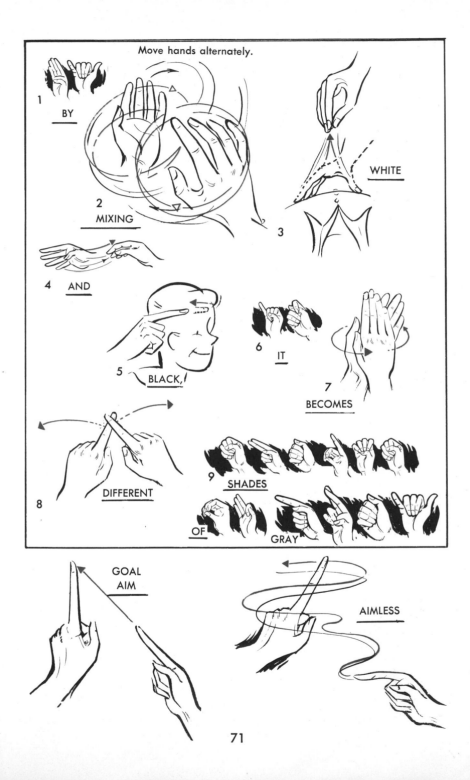

Move hands alternately.

1 BY

2 MIXING

3 WHITE

4 AND

5 BLACK,

6 IT

7 BECOMES

8 DIFFERENT

9 SHADES OF GRAY

GOAL AIM

AIMLESS

71

Time

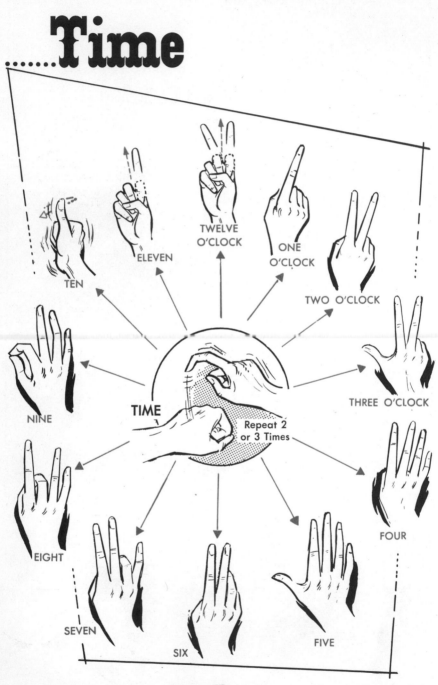

TEN

ELEVEN

TWELVE O'CLOCK

ONE O'CLOCK

TWO O'CLOCK

THREE O'CLOCK

NINE

TIME

Repeat 2 or 3 Times

FOUR

EIGHT

SEVEN

SIX

FIVE

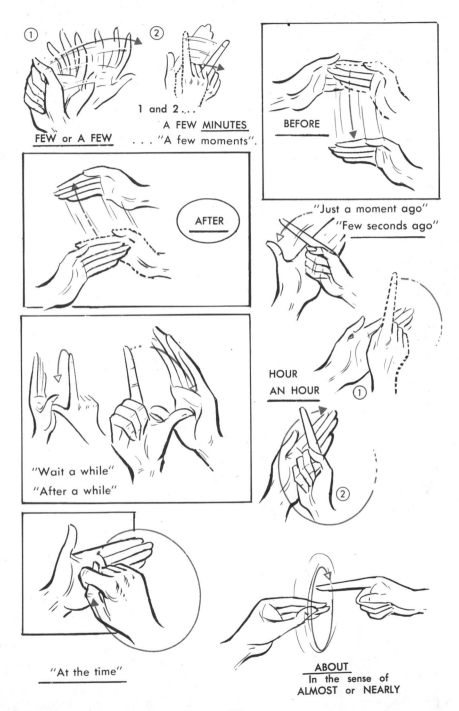

① ②

1 and 2 ...
A FEW <u>MINUTES</u>
... "A few moments".

<u>FEW or A FEW</u>

<u>BEFORE</u>

<u>AFTER</u>

"Just a moment ago"
"Few seconds ago"

HOUR
<u>AN HOUR</u>
①
②

"Wait a while"
"After a while"

"At the time"

<u>ABOUT</u>
In the sense of
ALMOST or NEARLY

73

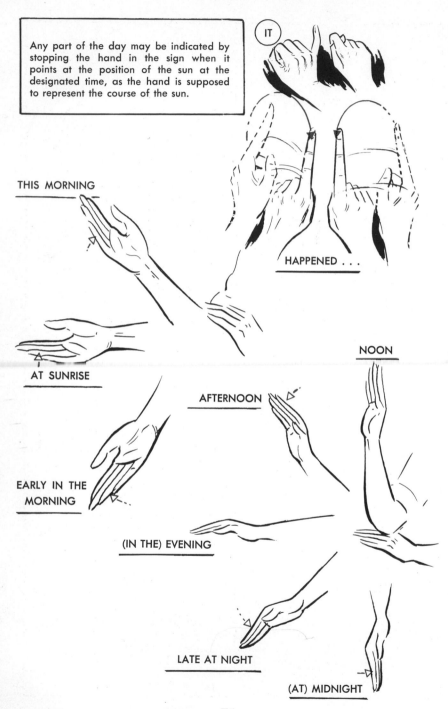

Any part of the day may be indicated by stopping the hand in the sign when it points at the position of the sun at the designated time, as the hand is supposed to represent the course of the sun.

IT

HAPPENED . . .

THIS MORNING

AT SUNRISE

NOON

AFTERNOON

EARLY IN THE MORNING

(IN THE) EVENING

LATE AT NIGHT

(AT) MIDNIGHT

74

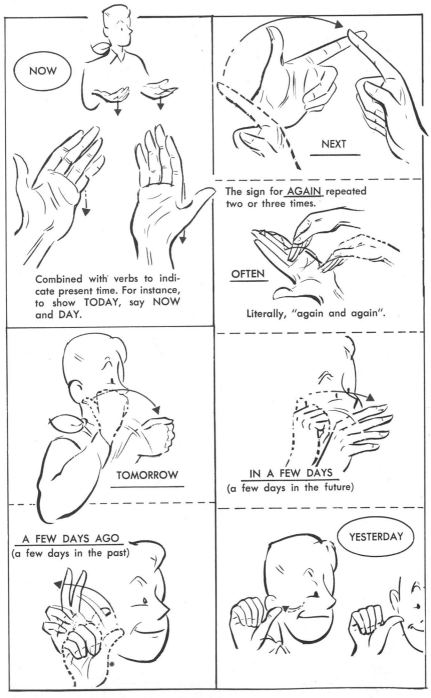

NOW

Combined with verbs to indicate present time. For instance, to show TODAY, say NOW and DAY.

NEXT

The sign for AGAIN repeated two or three times.

OFTEN

Literally, "again and again".

TOMORROW

IN A FEW DAYS
(a few days in the future)

A FEW DAYS AGO
(a few days in the past)

YESTERDAY

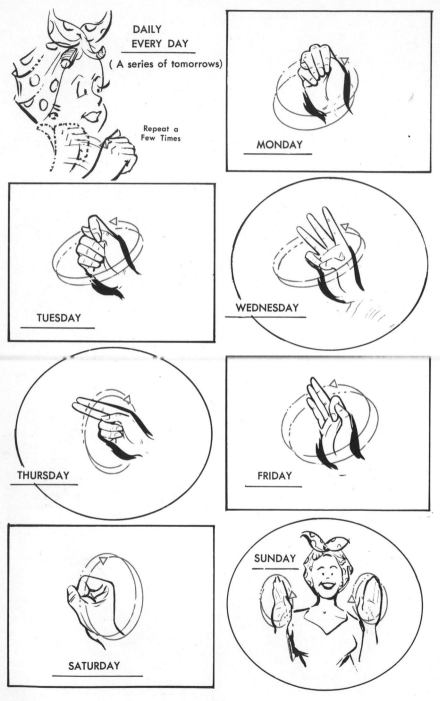

DAILY
EVERY DAY

(A series of tomorrows)

Repeat a
Few Times

MONDAY

TUESDAY

WEDNESDAY

THURSDAY

FRIDAY

SATURDAY

SUNDAY

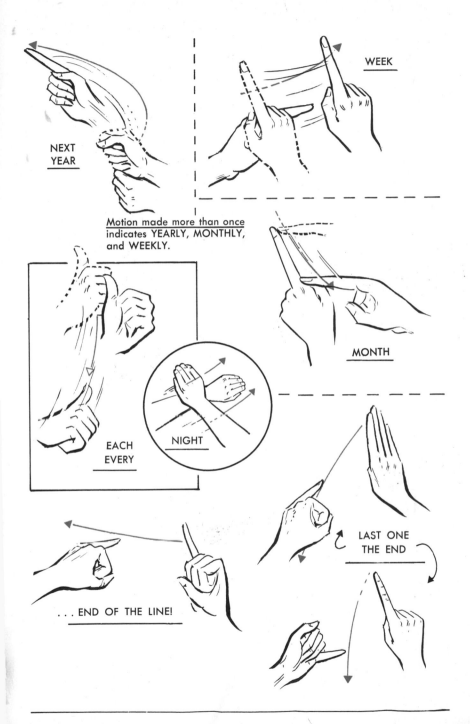

NEXT
YEAR

WEEK

Motion made more than once
indicates YEARLY, MONTHLY,
and WEEKLY.

MONTH

EACH
EVERY

NIGHT

LAST ONE
THE END

. . . END OF THE LINE!

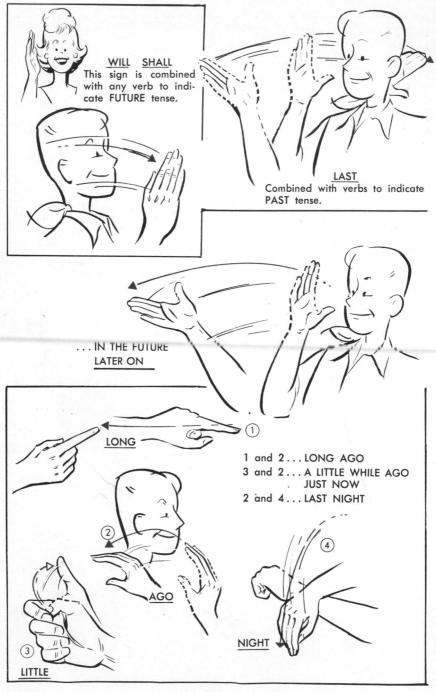

WILL SHALL
This sign is combined with any verb to indicate FUTURE tense.

LAST
Combined with verbs to indicate PAST tense.

...IN THE FUTURE
LATER ON

LONG

1 and 2 ... LONG AGO
3 and 2 ... A LITTLE WHILE AGO
            . JUST NOW
2 and 4 ... LAST NIGHT

AGO

LITTLE

NIGHT

HOLIDAY . . .

CHRISTMAS

Santa Claus

Describing the arc of a Christmas wreath

HAPPY

NEW

YEAR !

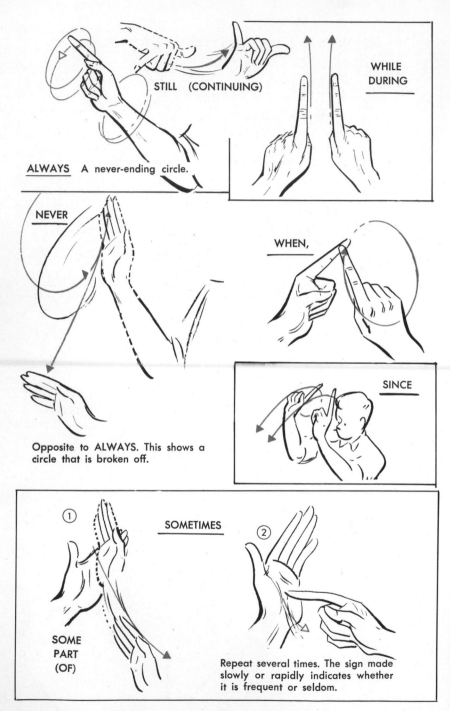

STILL   (CONTINUING)

WHILE
DURING

ALWAYS   A never-ending circle.

NEVER

WHEN,

SINCE

Opposite to ALWAYS. This shows a
circle that is broken off.

① SOMETIMES ②

SOME
PART
(OF)

Repeat several times. The sign made
slowly or rapidly indicates whether
it is frequent or seldom.

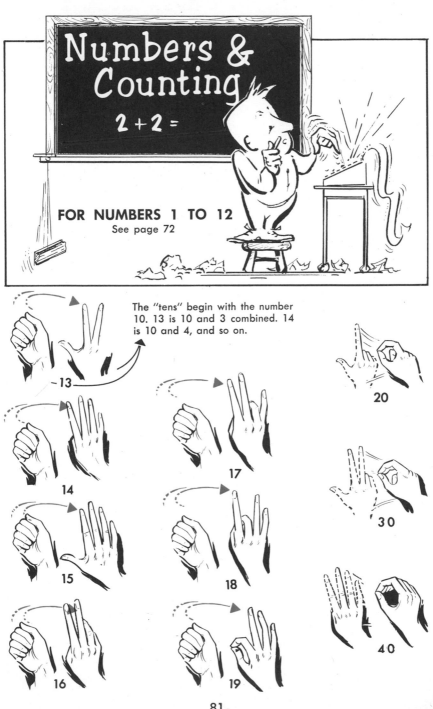

Numbers & Counting

$2 + 2 =$

FOR NUMBERS 1 TO 12
See page 72

The "tens" begin with the number 10. 13 is 10 and 3 combined. 14 is 10 and 4, and so on.

13

14

15

16

17

18

19

20

30

40

81

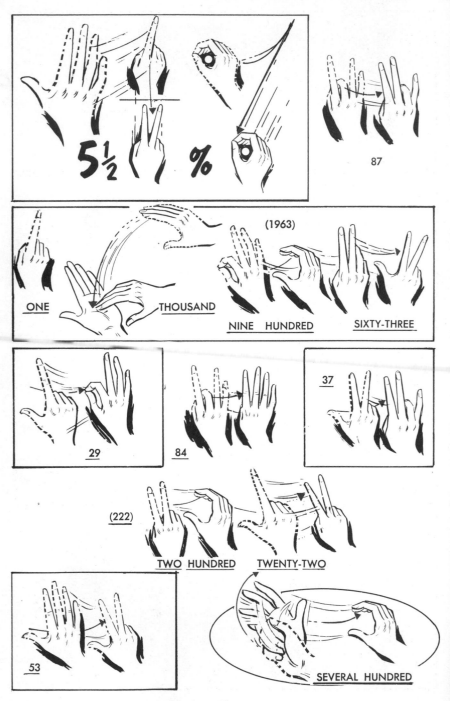

$5\frac{1}{2}$ (%

87

ONE THOUSAND (1963) NINE HUNDRED SIXTY-THREE

29 84 37

(222) TWO HUNDRED TWENTY-TWO

53 SEVERAL HUNDRED

82

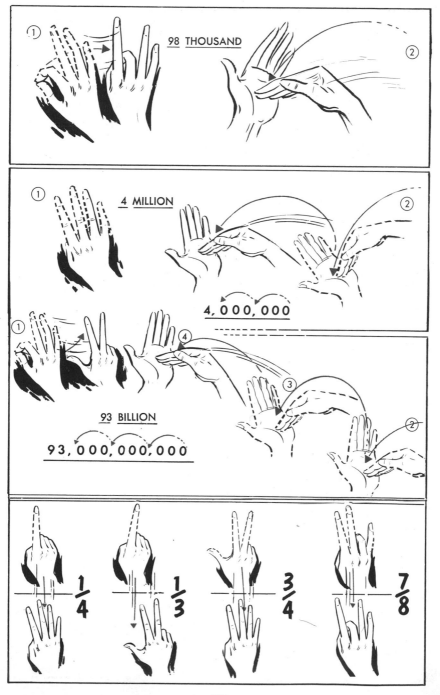

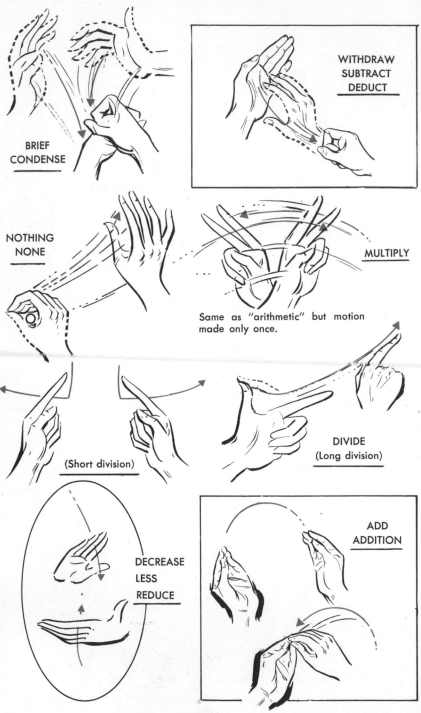

BRIEF
CONDENSE

WITHDRAW
SUBTRACT
DEDUCT

NOTHING
NONE

MULTIPLY

Same as "arithmetic" but motion
made only once.

(Short division)

DIVIDE
(Long division)

DECREASE
LESS
REDUCE

ADD
ADDITION

84

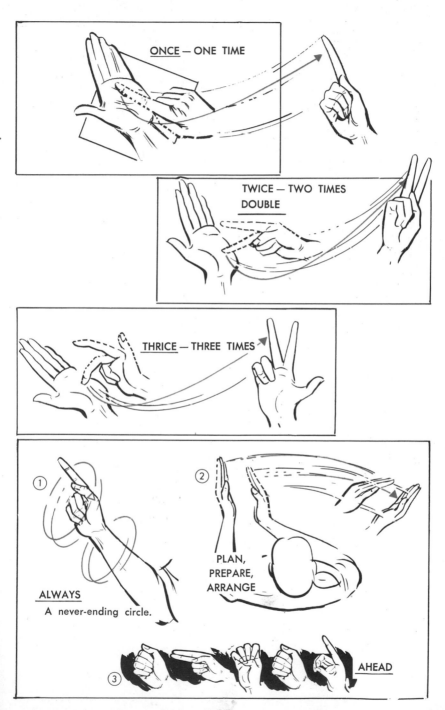

ONCE — ONE TIME

TWICE — TWO TIMES
DOUBLE

THRICE — THREE TIMES

① ALWAYS
A never-ending circle.

② PLAN,
PREPARE,
ARRANGE

③ AHEAD

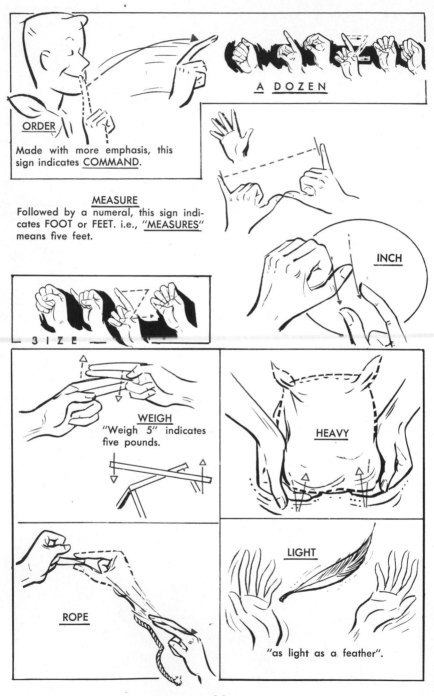

ORDER

Made with more emphasis, this sign indicates **COMMAND**.

A DOZEN

MEASURE

Followed by a numeral, this sign indicates **FOOT** or **FEET**. i.e., "**MEASURES**" means five feet.

INCH

S I Z E

WEIGH

"Weigh 5" indicates five pounds.

HEAVY

ROPE

LIGHT

"as light as a feather".

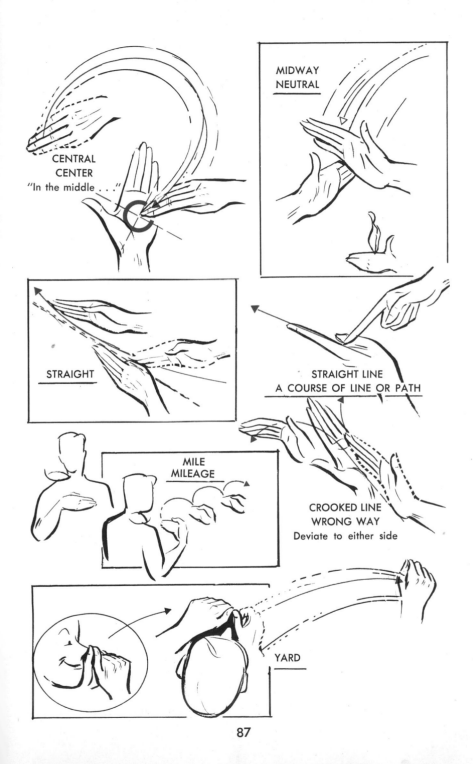

CENTRAL
CENTER
"In the middle . . ."

MIDWAY
NEUTRAL

STRAIGHT

STRAIGHT LINE
A COURSE OF LINE OR PATH

MILE
MILEAGE

CROOKED LINE
WRONG WAY
Deviate to either side

YARD

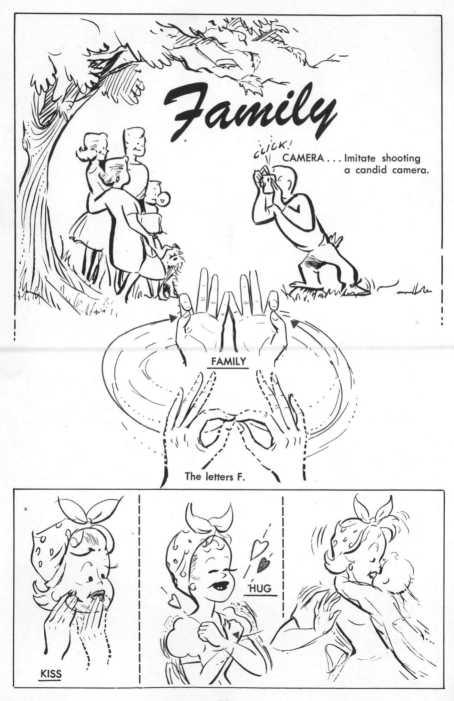

Family

CAMERA . . . Imitate shooting a candid camera.

CLICK!

FAMILY

The letters F.

KISS

HUG

GIRL

The sign indicates *female* sex and is the basic sign for woman, mother, lady, etc., as will be seen. It comes from the old days when women wore sunbonnets. The thumb drawn across the side of the face traces the bonnet ribbon.

<u>Male.</u> The sign indicates a man tipping his hat.

BOY

MOTHER

This is the sign for BABY. A mother is a girl (or female) who holds a baby, a combination of the sign for GIRL and BABY.

1 and 3 . . . MOTHER
2 and 3 . . . FATHER
1 and 4 . . . GRANDMOTHER
2 and 4 . . . GRANDFATHER

(See page <u>173</u>)

A <u>FATHER</u> is a male who holds a baby

A <u>GRANDMOTHER</u> is a female who has held two babies so the sign for BABY is made twice.

<u>GRANDFATHER</u> holds two babies.

1 and 3 . . . SON
2 and 3 . . . DAUGHTER

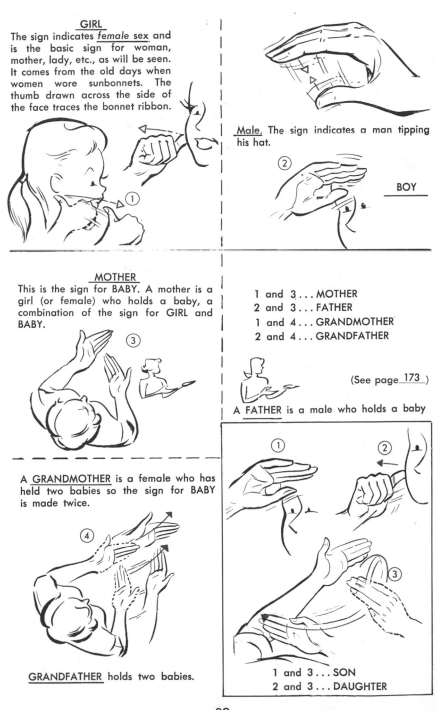

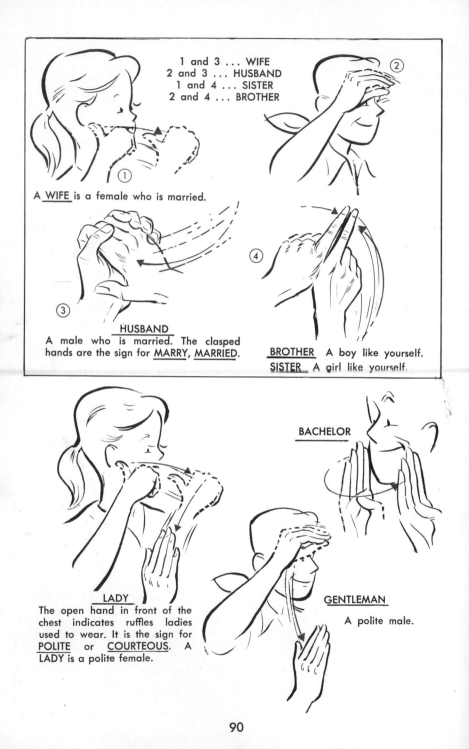

1 and 3 ... WIFE
2 and 3 ... HUSBAND
1 and 4 ... SISTER
2 and 4 ... BROTHER

A **WIFE** is a female who is married.

HUSBAND
A male who is married. The clasped
hands are the sign for **MARRY, MARRIED.**

BROTHER A boy like yourself.
SISTER A girl like yourself.

BACHELOR

LADY
The open hand in front of the
chest indicates ruffles ladies
used to wear. It is the sign for
POLITE or **COURTEOUS.** A
LADY is a polite female.

GENTLEMAN

A polite male.

90

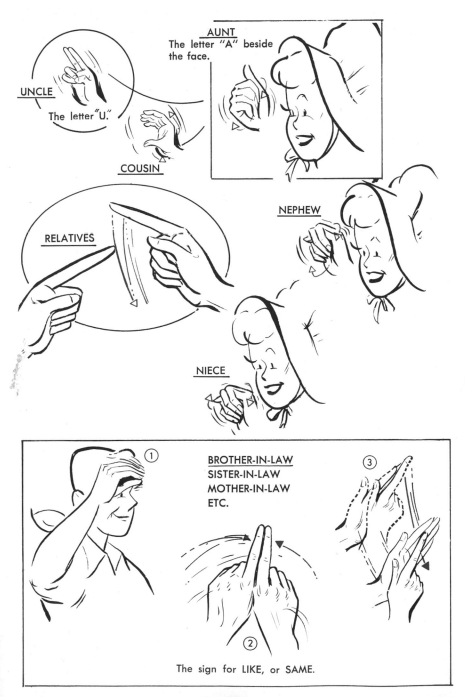

UNCLE
The letter "U."

AUNT
The letter "A" beside the face.

COUSIN

RELATIVES

NEPHEW

NIECE

BROTHER-IN-LAW
SISTER-IN-LAW
MOTHER-IN-LAW
ETC.

① ② ③

The sign for LIKE, or SAME.

CHURCH CHAPEL

RELIGION

Religion

GOD

WORSHIP

(Showing the scars on His hands.)

JESUS

① ②

③

HOLY

THE BIBLE (Jesus' Book)

SPIRIT SOUL (also GHOST)

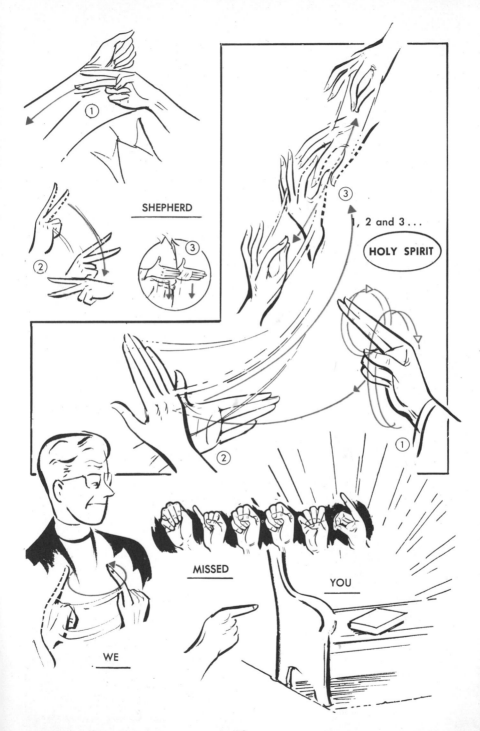

SHEPHERD

1, 2 and 3 . . .

HOLY SPIRIT

WE

MISSED

YOU

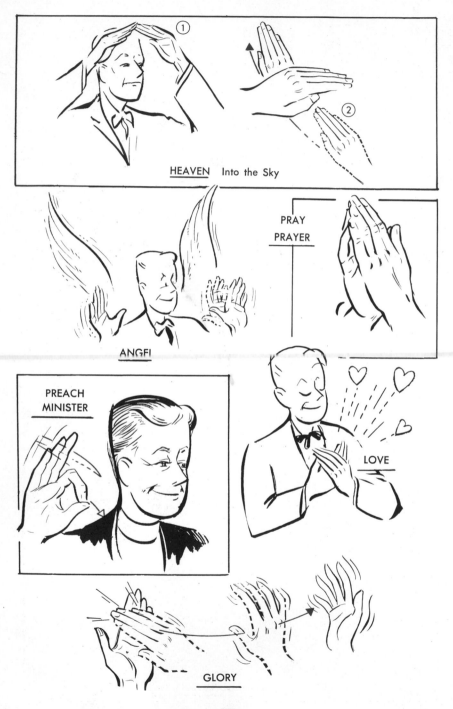

HEAVEN Into the Sky

PRAY
PRAYER

ANGEL

PREACH
MINISTER

LOVE

GLORY

94

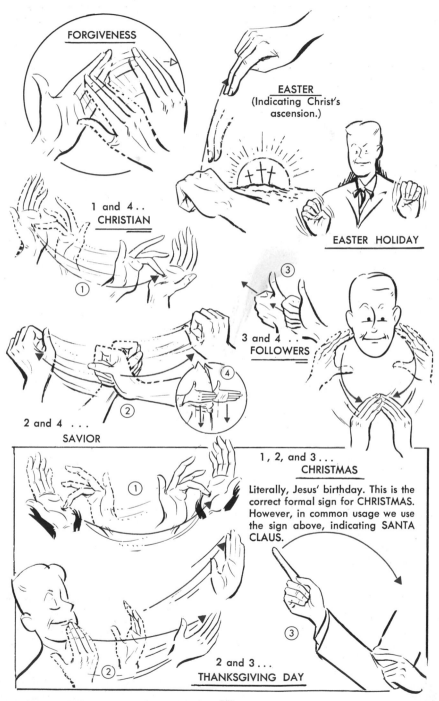

FORGIVENESS

EASTER
(Indicating Christ's
ascension.)

EASTER HOLIDAY

1 and 4..
CHRISTIAN

3 and 4 ..
FOLLOWERS

2 and 4 . . .
SAVIOR

1, 2, and 3 . . .
CHRISTMAS

Literally, Jesus' birthday. This is the correct formal sign for CHRISTMAS. However, in common usage we use the sign above, indicating SANTA CLAUS.

2 and 3 . . .
THANKSGIVING DAY

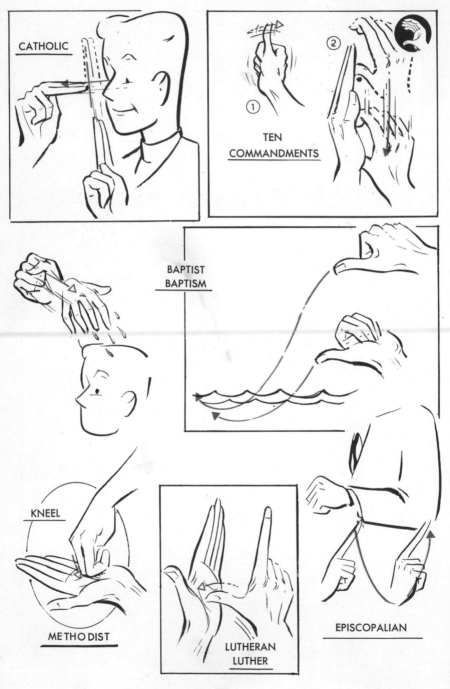

CATHOLIC

TEN COMMANDMENTS

① ②

BAPTIST BAPTISM

KNEEL

METHODIST

LUTHERAN LUTHER

EPISCOPALIAN

96

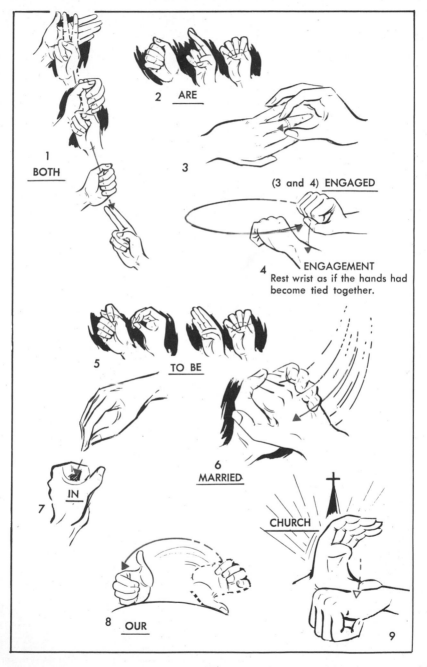

1
BOTH

2 ARE

3

(3 and 4) ENGAGED

4 ENGAGEMENT
Rest wrist as if the hands had
become tied together.

5

TO BE

6
MARRIED

7 IN

CHURCH

8 OUR

9

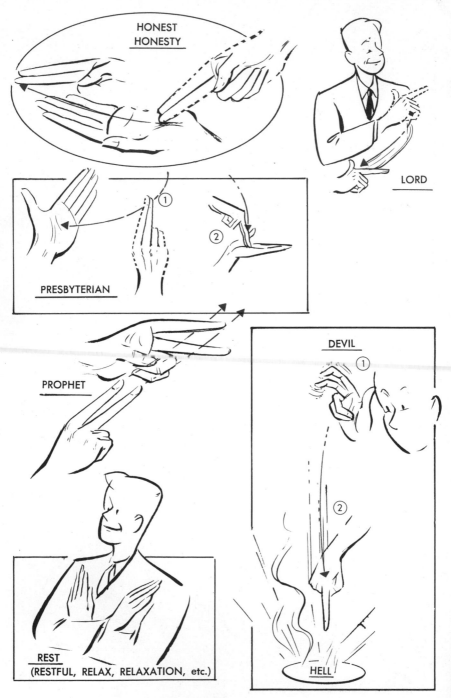

HONEST
HONESTY

LORD

PRESBYTERIAN

PROPHET

DEVIL

REST
(RESTFUL, RELAX, RELAXATION, etc.)

HELL

98

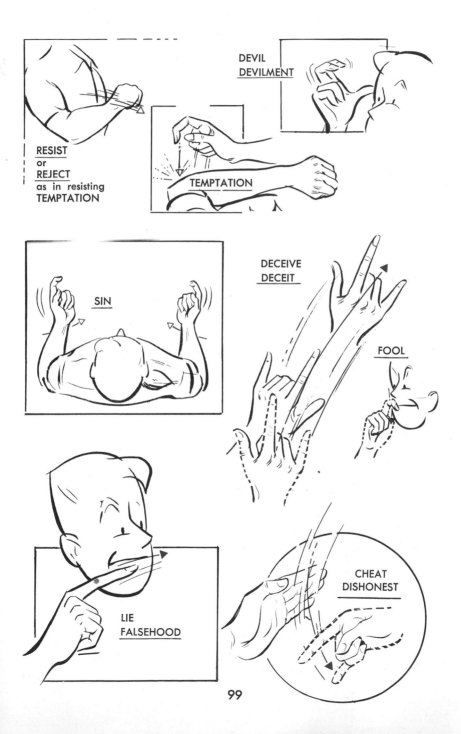

RESIST or REJECT as in resisting TEMPTATION

DEVIL DEVILMENT

TEMPTATION

SIN

DECEIVE DECEIT

FOOL

LIE FALSEHOOD

CHEAT DISHONEST

99

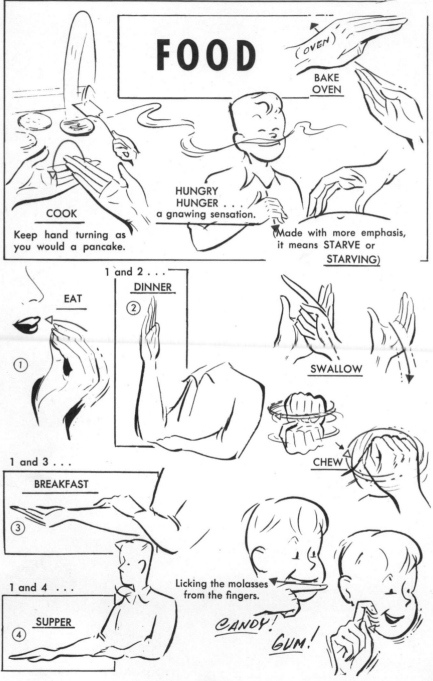

FOOD

BAKE OVEN (OVEN)

COOK
Keep hand turning as you would a pancake.

HUNGRY HUNGER . . . a gnawing sensation.

(Made with more emphasis, it means STARVE or STARVING)

EAT

1 and 2 . . .
DINNER

SWALLOW

CHEW

1 and 3 . . .
BREAKFAST

1 and 4 . . .
SUPPER

Licking the molasses from the fingers.

CANDY!

GUM!

100

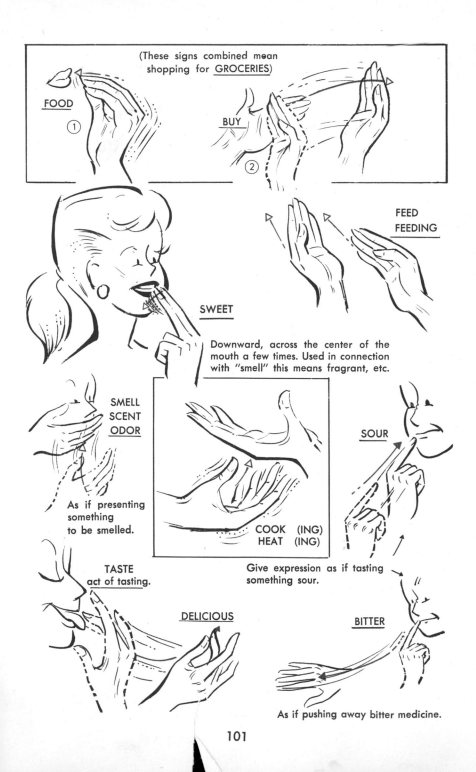

(These signs combined mean shopping for GROCERIES)

FOOD
①

BUY
②

FEED
FEEDING

SWEET

Downward, across the center of the mouth a few times. Used in connection with "smell" this means fragrant, etc.

SMELL
SCENT
ODOR

As if presenting something to be smelled.

COOK (ING)
HEAT (ING)

SOUR

Give expression as if tasting something sour.

TASTE
act of tasting.

DELICIOUS

BITTER

As if pushing away bitter medicine.

101

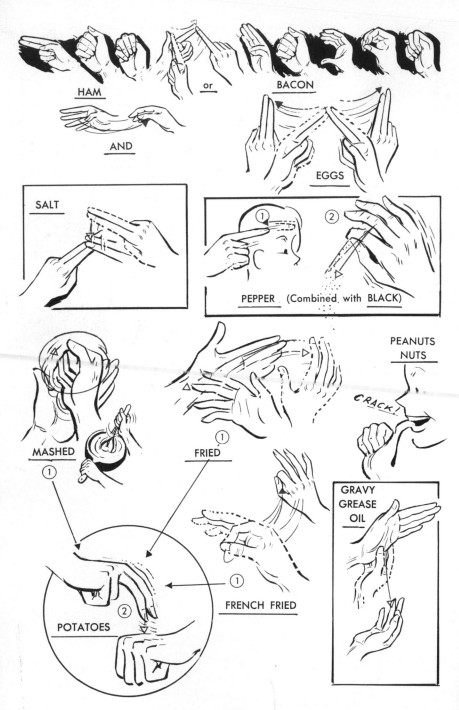

HAM   or   BACON

AND

EGGS

SALT

PEPPER (Combined with BLACK)

MASHED
①

FRIED
①

PEANUTS
NUTS

CRACK!

POTATOES
②

FRENCH FRIED
①

GRAVY
GREASE
OIL

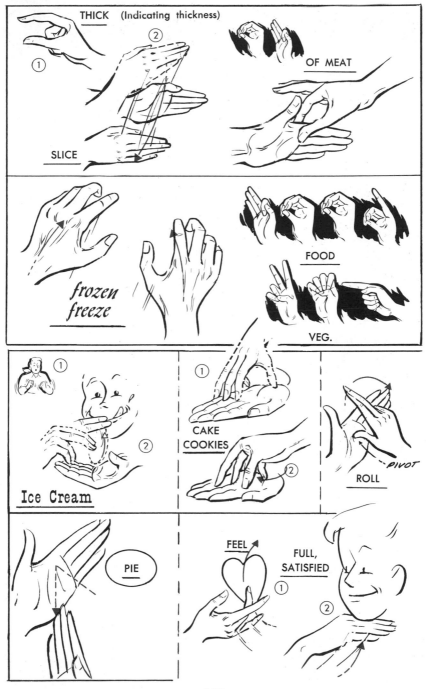

THICK (Indicating thickness)

① ②

SLICE

OF MEAT

frozen
freeze

FOOD

VEG.

① ②

Ice Cream

① CAKE COOKIES ②

ROLL

PIVOT

PIE

FEEL

FULL, SATISFIED

① ②

103

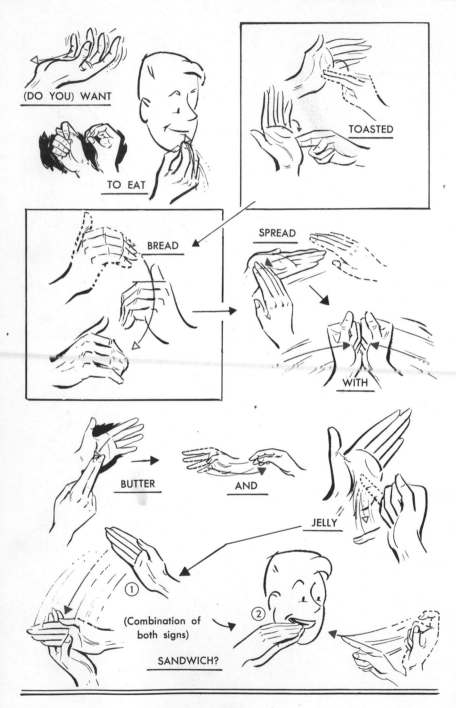

(DO YOU) WANT

TO EAT

TOASTED

BREAD

SPREAD

WITH

BUTTER

AND

JELLY

① (Combination of both signs) → ②

SANDWICH?

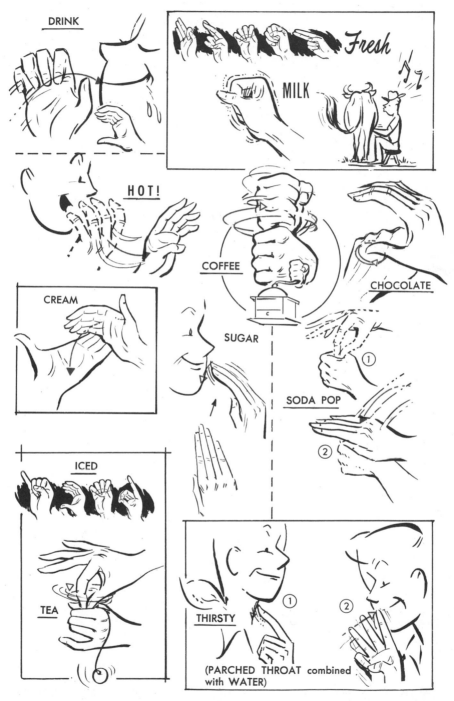

DRINK

Fresh

MILK

HOT!

COFFEE

CHOCOLATE

CREAM

SUGAR

SODA POP
①
②

ICED

TEA

THIRSTY ① ②

(PARCHED THROAT combined
with WATER)

105

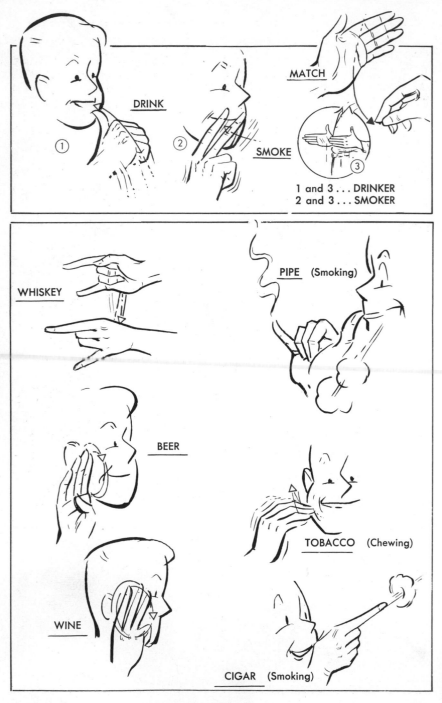

DRINK

①

MATCH

②

SMOKE

③

1 and 3 ... DRINKER
2 and 3 ... SMOKER

WHISKEY

PIPE (Smoking)

BEER

TOBACCO (Chewing)

WINE

CIGAR (Smoking)

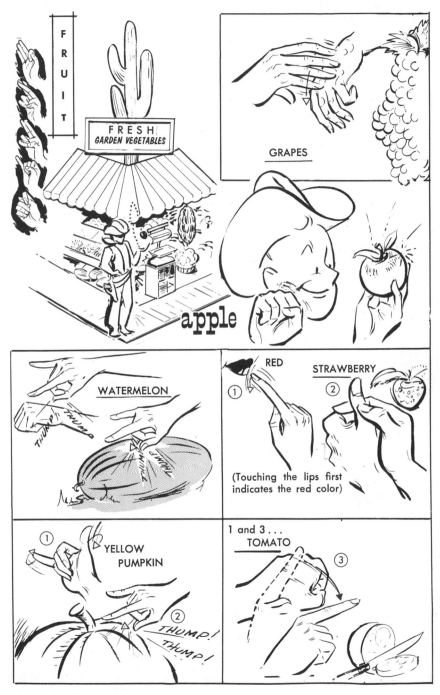

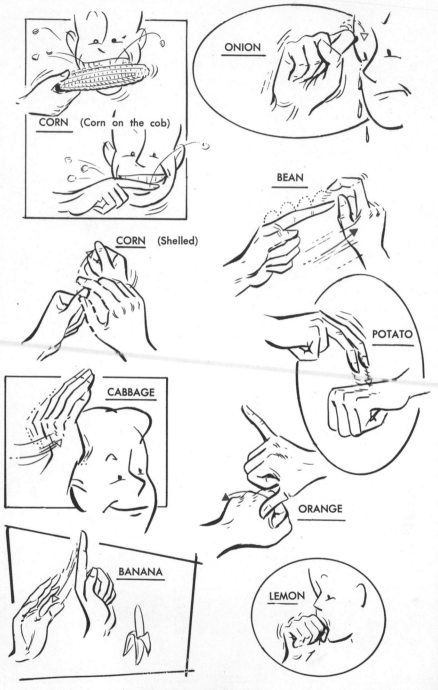

CORN (Corn on the cob)

ONION

CORN (Shelled)

BEAN

POTATO

CABBAGE

ORANGE

BANANA

LEMON

108

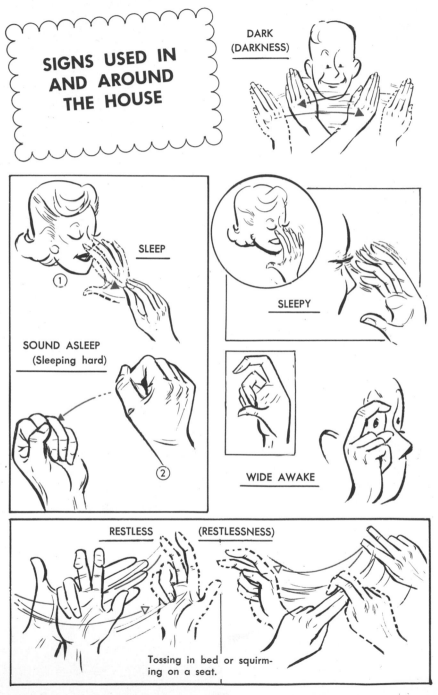

SIGNS USED IN AND AROUND THE HOUSE

DARK (DARKNESS)

SLEEP

SLEEPY

SOUND ASLEEP (Sleeping hard)

WIDE AWAKE

RESTLESS (RESTLESSNESS)

Tossing in bed or squirming on a seat.

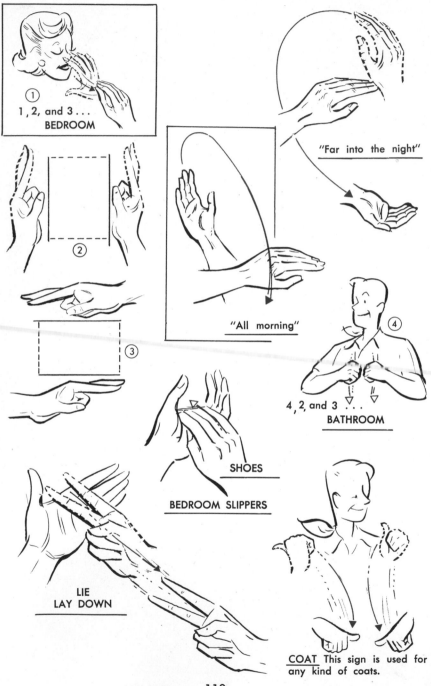

1, 2, and 3...
BEDROOM

①

②

③

"Far into the night"

"All morning"

4, 2, and 3...
BATHROOM

④

SHOES
BEDROOM SLIPPERS

LIE
LAY DOWN

COAT This sign is used for
any kind of coats.

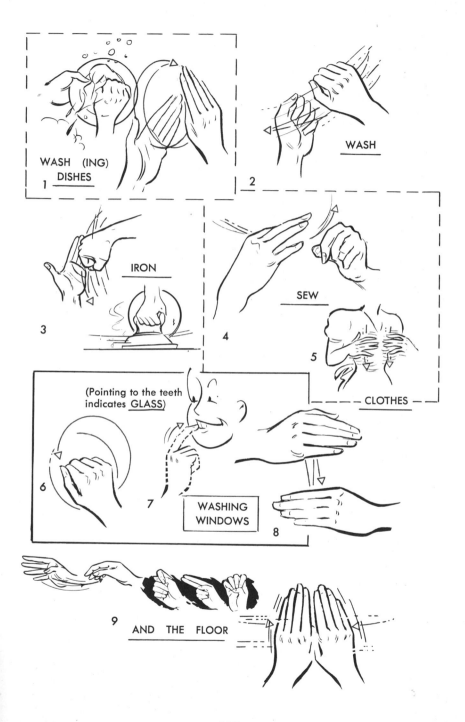

WASH (ING) DISHES
1

WASH
2

IRON
3

SEW
4

CLOTHES
5

(Pointing to the teeth indicates GLASS)
6

WASHING WINDOWS
7

8

AND THE FLOOR
9

111

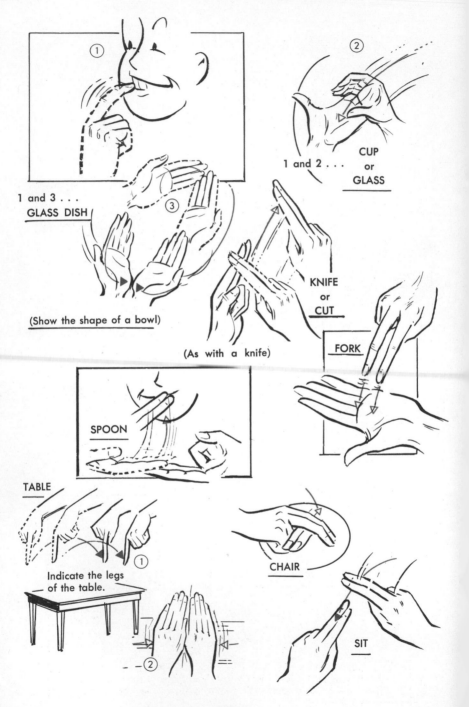

①

②

1 and 3 . . .
__GLASS DISH__

③

1 and 2 . . . CUP
or
GLASS

(Show the shape of a bowl)

KNIFE
or
__CUT__

(As with a knife)

__FORK__

__SPOON__

__TABLE__

Indicate the legs
of the table.

①

②

__CHAIR__

__SIT__

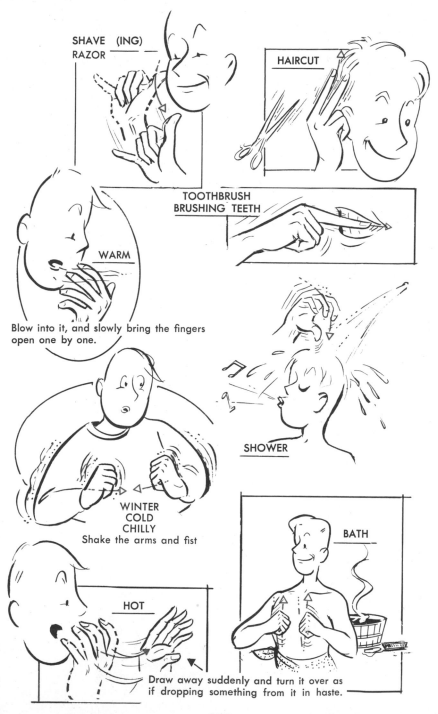

SHAVE (ING)
RAZOR

HAIRCUT

TOOTHBRUSH
BRUSHING TEETH

WARM

Blow into it, and slowly bring the fingers
open one by one.

SHOWER

WINTER
COLD
CHILLY
Shake the arms and fist

BATH

HOT

Draw away suddenly and turn it over as
if dropping something from it in haste.

113

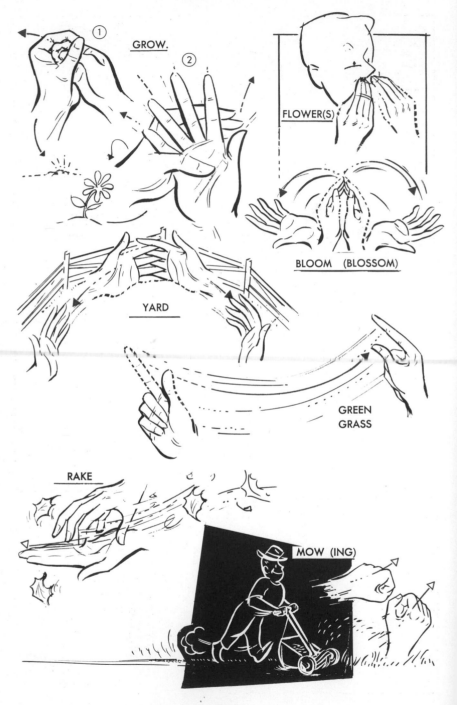

GROW.
①
②

FLOWER(S)

BLOOM (BLOSSOM)

YARD

GREEN
GRASS

RAKE

MOW (ING)

114

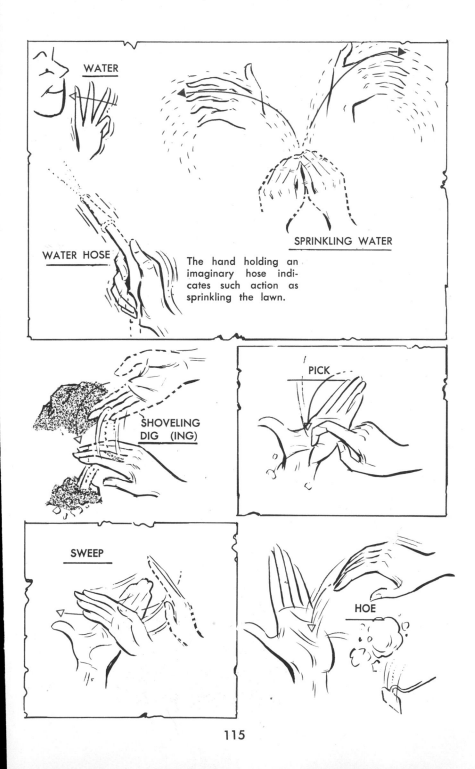

WATER

SPRINKLING WATER

WATER HOSE

The hand holding an imaginary hose indicates such action as sprinkling the lawn.

SHOVELING DIG (ING)

PICK

SWEEP

HOE

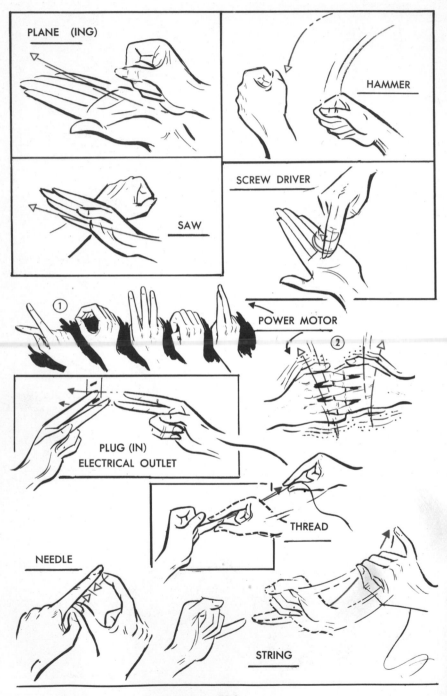

PLANE (ING)

HAMMER

SAW

SCREW DRIVER

POWER MOTOR

PLUG (IN)
ELECTRICAL OUTLET

THREAD

NEEDLE

STRING

116

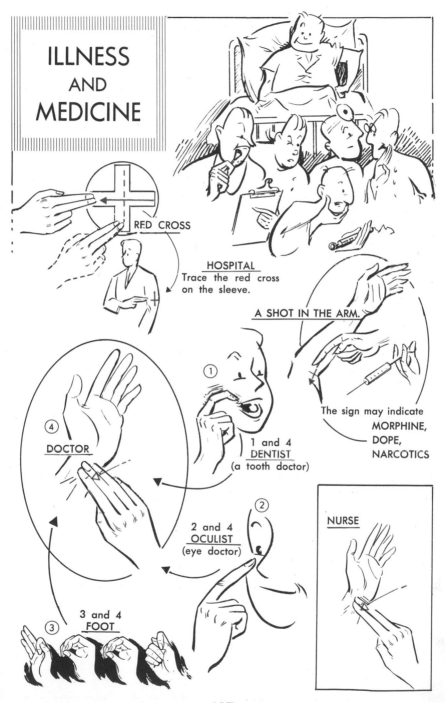

ILLNESS
AND
MEDICINE

RED CROSS

HOSPITAL
Trace the red cross
on the sleeve.

A SHOT IN THE ARM.

The sign may indicate
MORPHINE,
DOPE,
NARCOTICS

④
DOCTOR

①
1 and 4
DENTIST
(a tooth doctor)

②
2 and 4
OCULIST
(eye doctor)

NURSE

③
3 and 4
FOOT

117

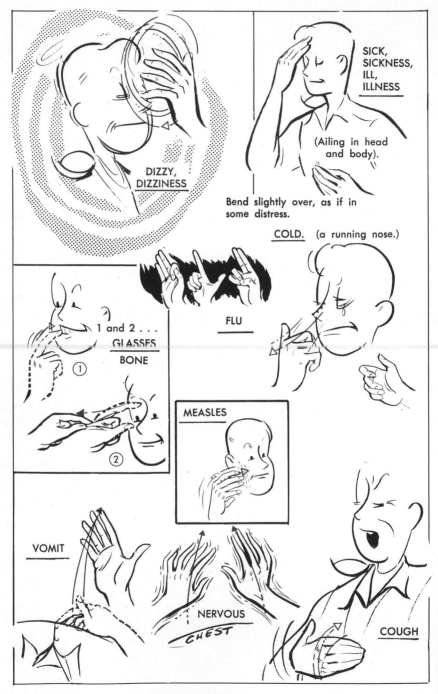

DIZZY, DIZZINESS

SICK, SICKNESS, ILL, ILLNESS

(Ailing in head and body).

Bend slightly over, as if in some distress.

COLD. (a running nose.)

1 and 2 . . .
GLASSES
BONE

FLU

MEASLES

VOMIT

NERVOUS

CHEST

COUGH

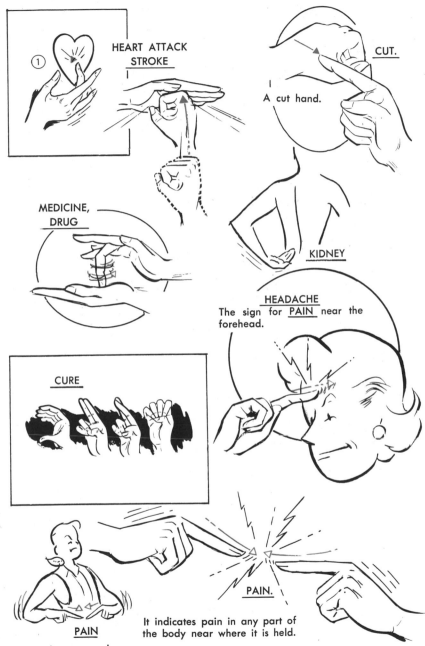

HEART ATTACK
STROKE

① CUT.

A cut hand.

MEDICINE, DRUG

KIDNEY

HEADACHE
The sign for PAIN near the forehead.

CURE

PAIN
A tummy ache.

PAIN.
It indicates pain in any part of the body near where it is held.

119

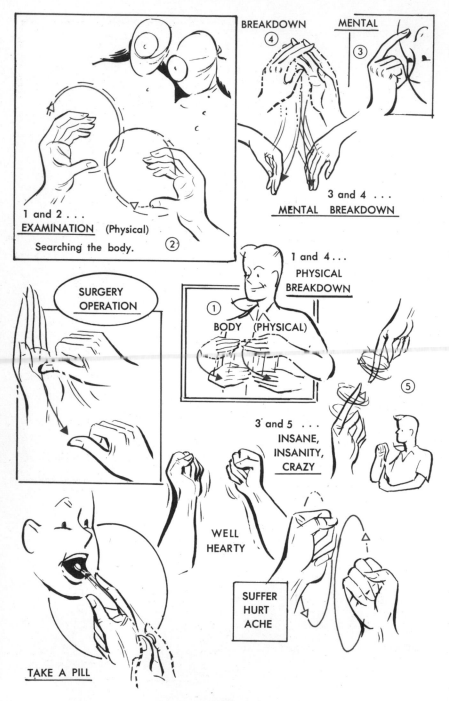

1 and 2 . . .
EXAMINATION (Physical)
Searching the body. ②

BREAKDOWN ④

MENTAL ③

3 and 4 . . .
MENTAL BREAKDOWN

1 and 4 . . .
PHYSICAL BREAKDOWN

① BODY (PHYSICAL)

SURGERY OPERATION

⑤

3 and 5 . . .
INSANE, INSANITY, CRAZY

WELL HEARTY

SUFFER HURT ACHE

TAKE A PILL

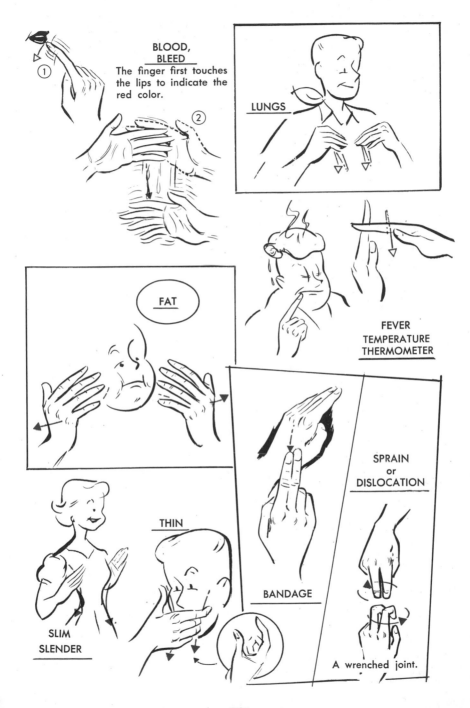

BLOOD,
BLEED
The finger first touches the lips to indicate the red color.

LUNGS

FAT

FEVER
TEMPERATURE
THERMOMETER

SPRAIN
or
DISLOCATION

THIN

BANDAGE

SLIM
SLENDER

A wrenched joint.

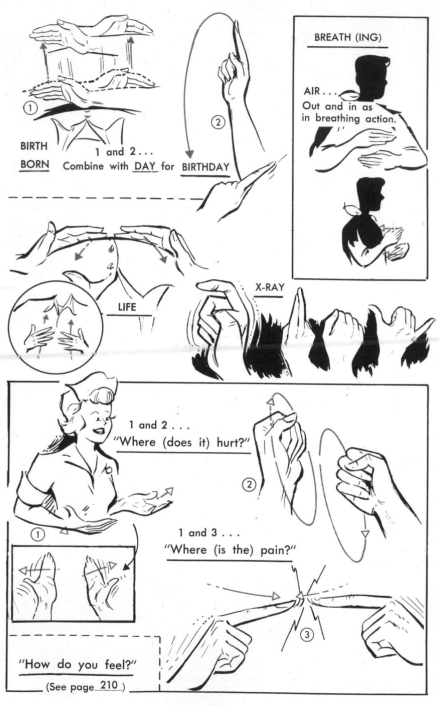

BIRTH
BORN

1 and 2 . . . Combine with <u>DAY</u> for <u>BIRTHDAY</u>

BREATH (ING)

AIR . . .
Out and in as in breathing action.

LIFE

X-RAY

1 and 2 . . .
"Where (does it) hurt?"

1 and 3 . . .
"Where (is the) pain?"

"How do you feel?"

(See page 210)

122

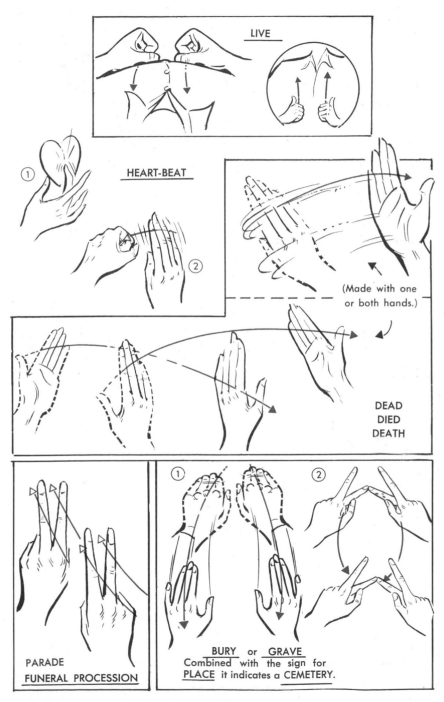

LIVE

HEART-BEAT

(Made with one
or both hands.)

DEAD
DIED
DEATH

PARADE
FUNERAL PROCESSION

BURY or GRAVE
Combined with the sign for
PLACE it indicates a CEMETERY.

123

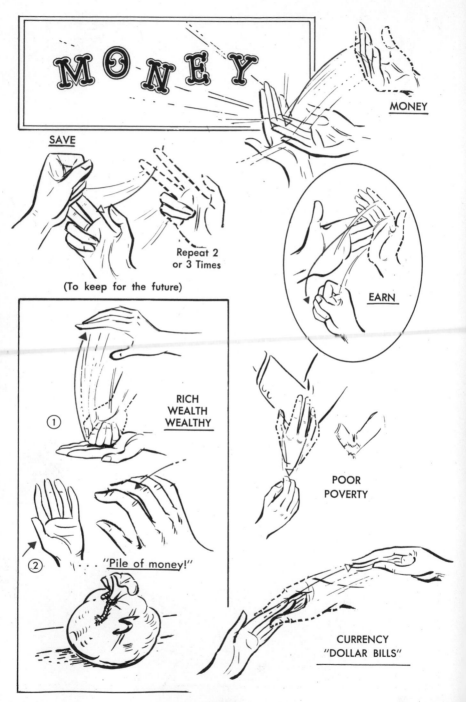

MONEY

MONEY

SAVE

Repeat 2
or 3 Times

(To keep for the future)

EARN

RICH
WEALTH
WEALTHY

①

②

"Pile of money!"

POOR
POVERTY

CURRENCY
"DOLLAR BILLS"

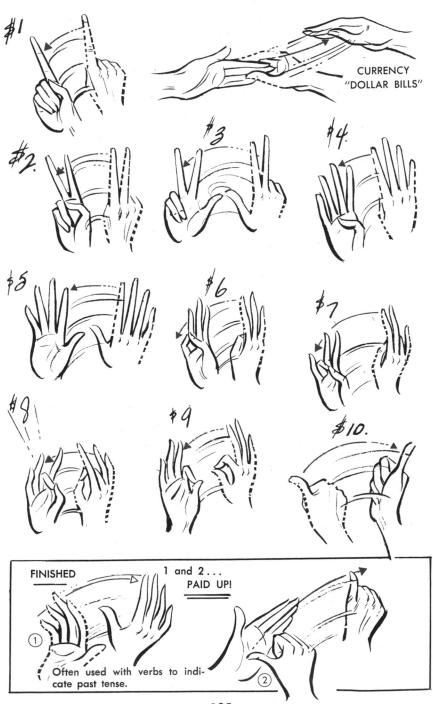

#1

CURRENCY
"DOLLAR BILLS"

#2.

#3

#4.

$5

$6

$7

$8

$9

$10.

FINISHED

1 and 2...
PAID UP!

①

②

Often used with verbs to indicate past tense.

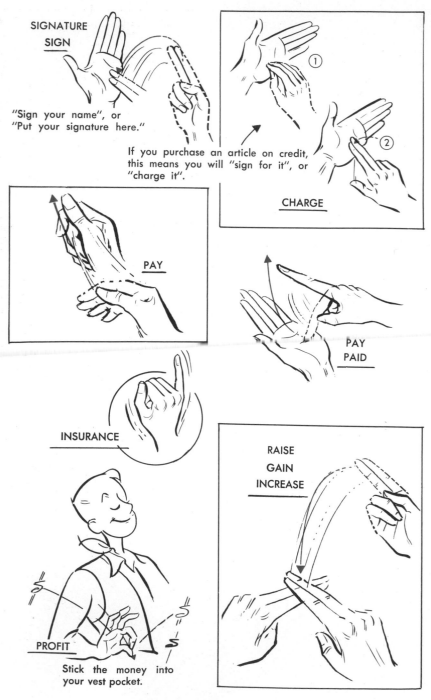

SIGNATURE
SIGN

"Sign your name", or
"Put your signature here."

If you purchase an article on credit,
this means you will "sign for it", or
"charge it".

①

②

CHARGE

PAY

PAY
PAID

INSURANCE

RAISE
GAIN
INCREASE

PROFIT

Stick the money into
your vest pocket.

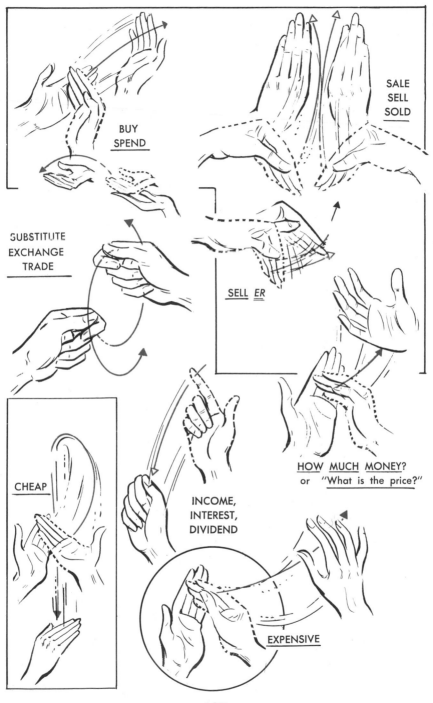

BUY
SPEND

SALE
SELL
SOLD

SUBSTITUTE
EXCHANGE
TRADE

SELL *ER*

CHEAP

INCOME,
INTEREST,
DIVIDEND

HOW MUCH MONEY?
or "What is the price?"

EXPENSIVE

127

Repeated several times, or made with both hands
alternately, it means <u>WASTE</u> or <u>EXTRAVAGANCE.</u>
Spending much, or a lot of —

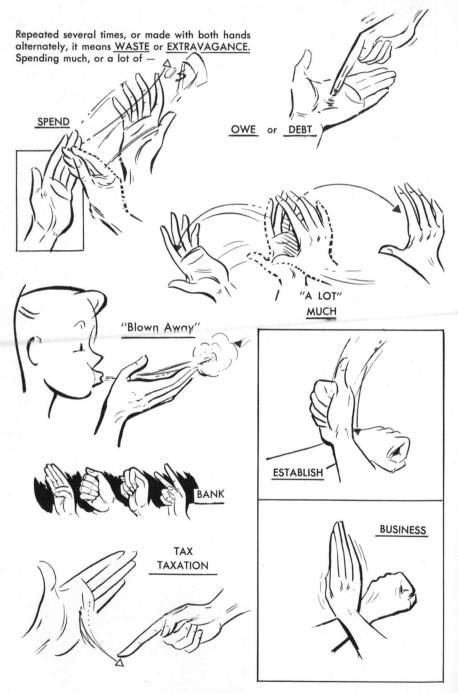

<u>SPEND</u>

<u>OWE</u> or <u>DEBT</u>

"A LOT"
<u>MUCH</u>

"Blown Away"

ESTABLISH

BANK

BUSINESS

TAX
<u>TAXATION</u>

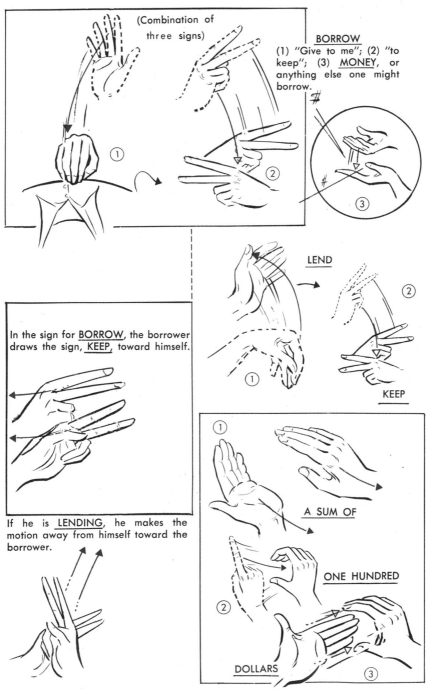

(Combination of three signs)

BORROW
(1) "Give to me"; (2) "to keep"; (3) MONEY, or anything else one might borrow.

In the sign for BORROW, the borrower draws the sign, KEEP, toward himself.

If he is LENDING, he makes the motion away from himself toward the borrower.

LEND

KEEP

A SUM OF

ONE HUNDRED

DOLLARS

OCCUPATIONS

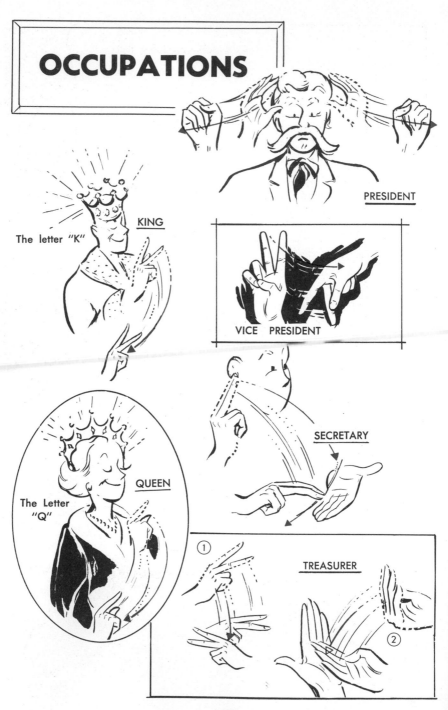

PRESIDENT

The letter "K"   KING

VICE PRESIDENT

SECRETARY

The Letter "Q"   QUEEN

TREASURER

① ②

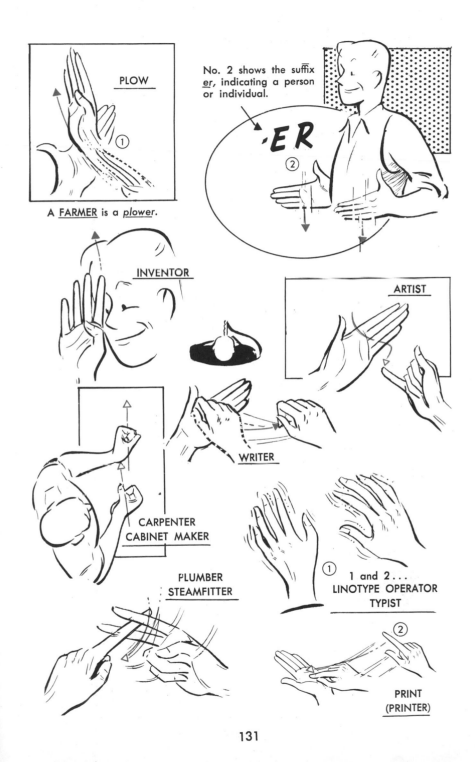

PLOW

A FARMER is a _plower_.

No. 2 shows the suffix _er_, indicating a person or individual.

ER

INVENTOR

ARTIST

WRITER

CARPENTER
CABINET MAKER

PLUMBER
STEAMFITTER

1 and 2...
LINOTYPE OPERATOR
TYPIST

PRINT
(PRINTER)

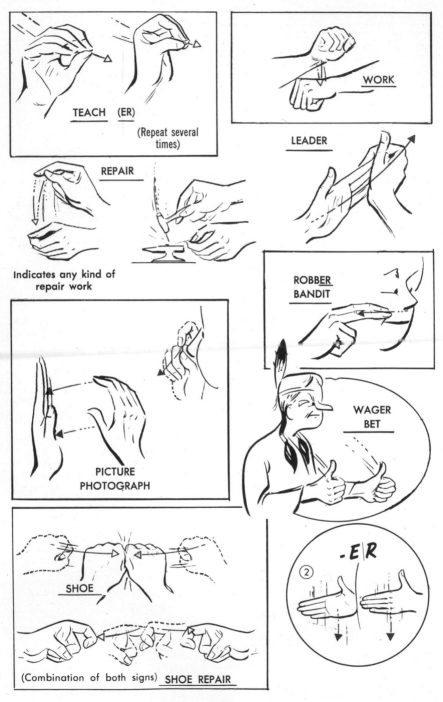

TEACH (ER)
(Repeat several times)

WORK

LEADER

REPAIR

Indicates any kind of repair work

ROBBER
BANDIT

WAGER
BET

PICTURE
PHOTOGRAPH

SHOE

-ER

②

(Combination of both signs) SHOE REPAIR

132

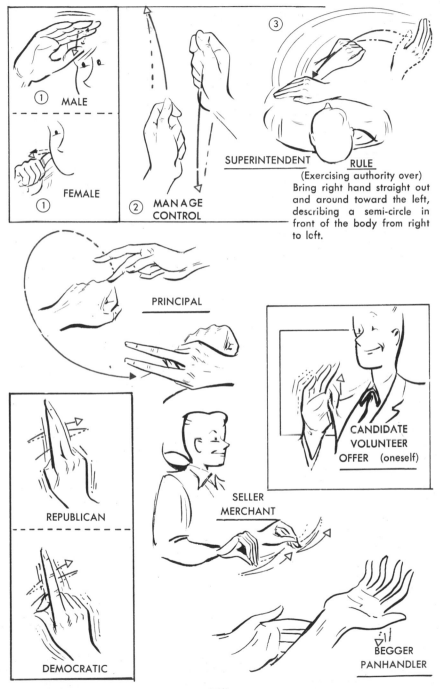

① MALE

① FEMALE

② MANAGE CONTROL

SUPERINTENDENT

RULE
(Exercising authority over)
Bring right hand straight out and around toward the left, describing a semi-circle in front of the body from right to left.

PRINCIPAL

REPUBLICAN

DEMOCRATIC

SELLER MERCHANT

CANDIDATE
VOLUNTEER
OFFER   (oneself)

BEGGER
PANHANDLER

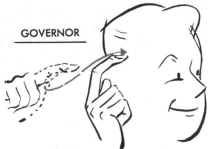

GOVERNOR

(This sign means CAPITAL, GOVERNMENT, GOVERNOR. It is used to denote several cities in the U.S. which are state capitals.)

LEGISLATURE

LECTURE, ADDRESS, SPEECH

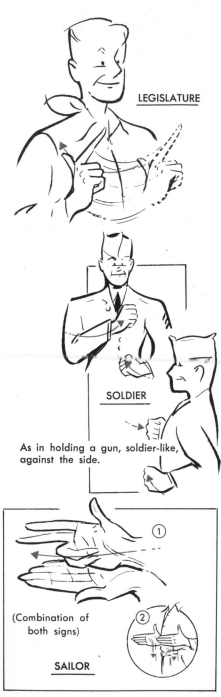

SOLDIER

As in holding a gun, soldier-like, against the side.

OFFICER CAPTAIN

(Combination of both signs)

SAILOR

①

②

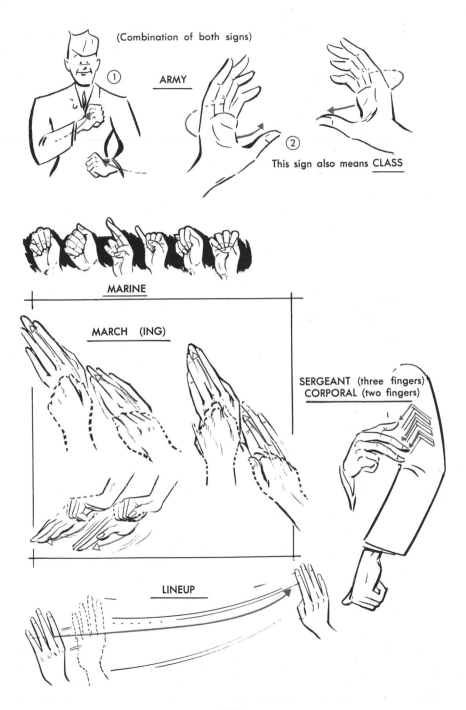

(Combination of both signs)

① ARMY

② This sign also means CLASS

MARINE

MARCH (ING)

SERGEANT (three fingers)
CORPORAL (two fingers)

LINEUP

135

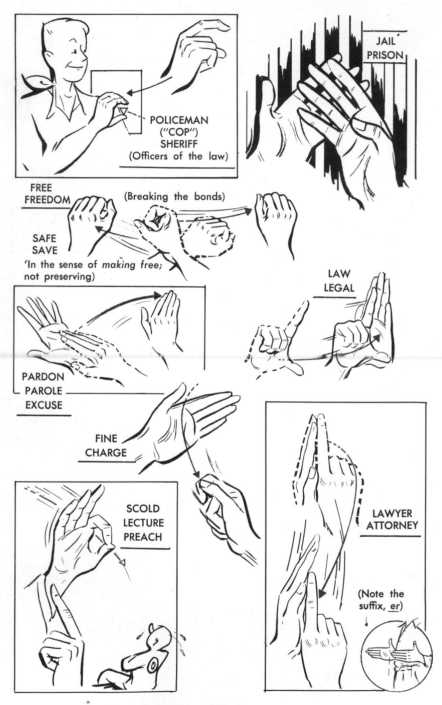

POLICEMAN
("COP")
SHERIFF
(Officers of the law)

JAIL
PRISON

FREE
FREEDOM

(Breaking the bonds)

SAFE
SAVE

'In the sense of *making free*;
not preserving)

PARDON
PAROLE
EXCUSE

LAW
LEGAL

FINE
CHARGE

SCOLD
LECTURE
PREACH

LAWYER
ATTORNEY

(Note the
suffix, er)

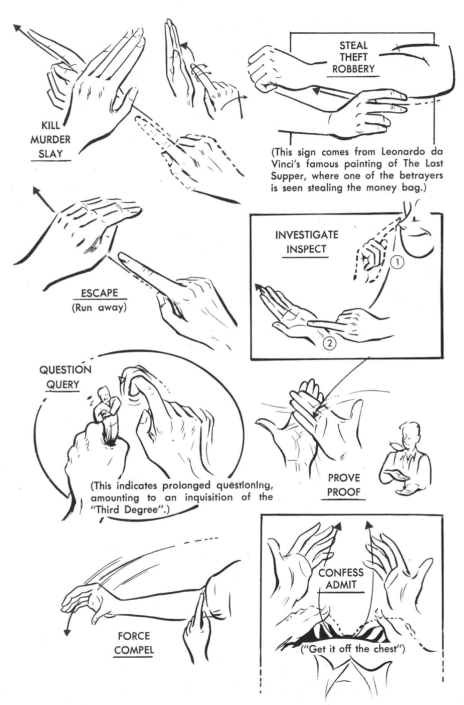

KILL
MURDER
SLAY

STEAL
THEFT
ROBBERY

(This sign comes from Leonardo da Vinci's famous painting of The Last Supper, where one of the betrayers is seen stealing the money bag.)

ESCAPE
(Run away)

INVESTIGATE
INSPECT
①
②

QUESTION
QUERY

(This indicates prolonged questioning, amounting to an inquisition of the "Third Degree".)

PROVE
PROOF

FORCE
COMPEL

CONFESS
ADMIT

("Get it off the chest")

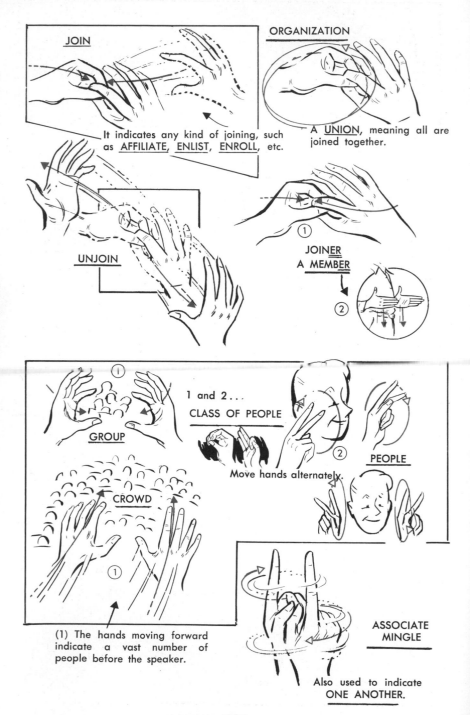

JOIN

It indicates any kind of joining, such as AFFILIATE, ENLIST, ENROLL, etc.

ORGANIZATION

A UNION, meaning all are joined together.

UNJOIN

JOINER
A MEMBER

①

②

GROUP

1 and 2...
CLASS OF PEOPLE

Move hands alternately.

PEOPLE

CROWD

①

(1) The hands moving forward indicate a vast number of people before the speaker.

ASSOCIATE
MINGLE

Also used to indicate
ONE ANOTHER.

138

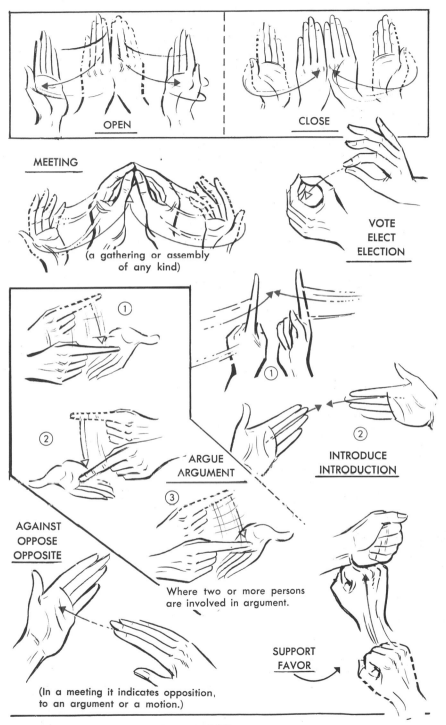

OPEN

CLOSE

MEETING

(a gathering or assembly
of any kind)

VOTE
ELECT
ELECTION

ARGUE
ARGUMENT

INTRODUCE
INTRODUCTION

AGAINST
OPPOSE
OPPOSITE

Where two or more persons
are involved in argument.

SUPPORT
FAVOR

(In a meeting it indicates opposition,
to an argument or a motion.)

139

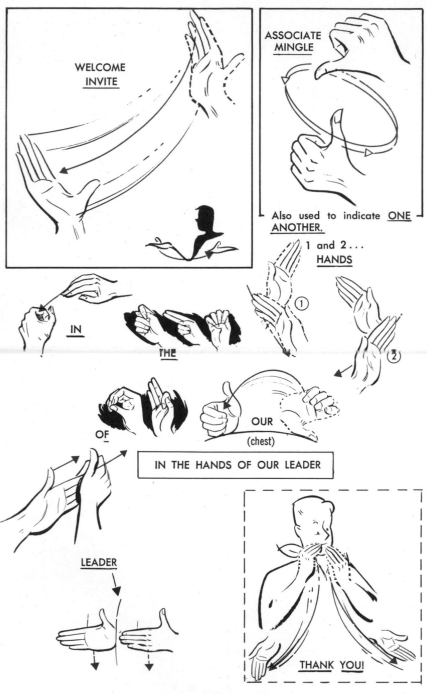

WELCOME
INVITE

ASSOCIATE
MINGLE

Also used to indicate ONE ANOTHER.

1 and 2 . . .
HANDS

IN

THE

OF

OUR
(chest)

IN THE HANDS OF OUR LEADER

LEADER

THANK YOU!

140

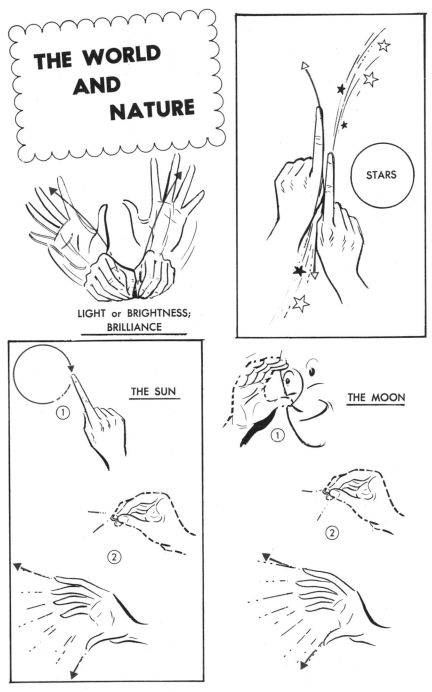

THE WORLD AND NATURE

LIGHT or BRIGHTNESS;
BRILLIANCE

STARS

THE SUN

THE MOON

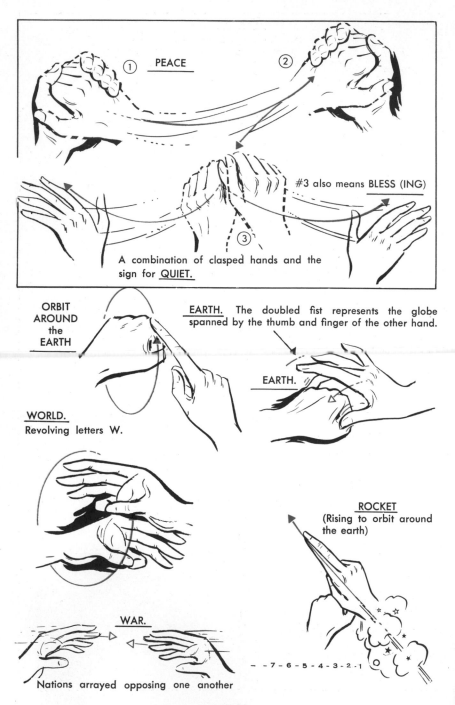

① PEACE

②

③
A combination of clasped hands and the
sign for QUIET.

#3 also means BLESS (ING)

ORBIT
AROUND
the
EARTH

EARTH. The doubled fist represents the globe
spanned by the thumb and finger of the other hand.

EARTH.

WORLD.
Revolving letters W.

ROCKET
(Rising to orbit around
the earth)

WAR.

Nations arrayed opposing one another

- - 7 - 6 - 5 - 4 - 3 - 2 - 1

142

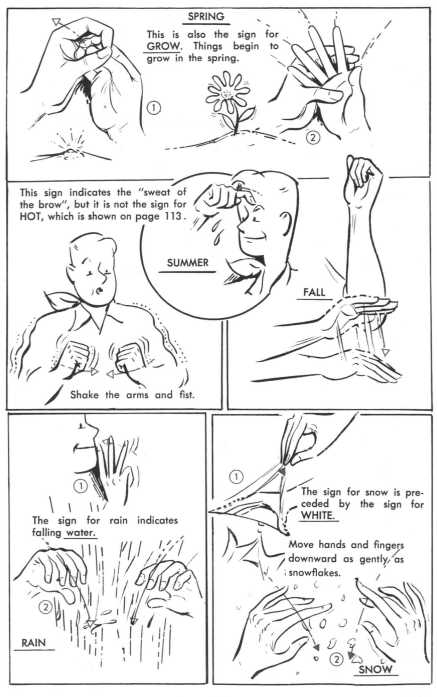

SPRING

This is also the sign for GROW. Things begin to grow in the spring.

①

②

This sign indicates the "sweat of the brow", but it is not the sign for HOT, which is shown on page 113.

SUMMER

FALL

Shake the arms and fist.

①

The sign for rain indicates falling water.

②

RAIN

①

The sign for snow is preceded by the sign for WHITE.

Move hands and fingers downward as gently as snowflakes.

②

SNOW

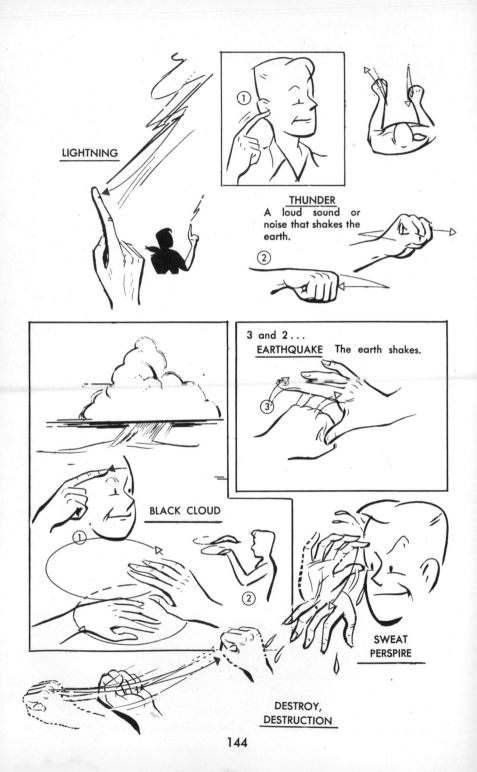

LIGHTNING

THUNDER
A loud sound or noise that shakes the earth.

3 and 2 . . .
EARTHQUAKE   The earth shakes.

BLACK CLOUD

SWEAT
PERSPIRE

DESTROY,
DESTRUCTION

144

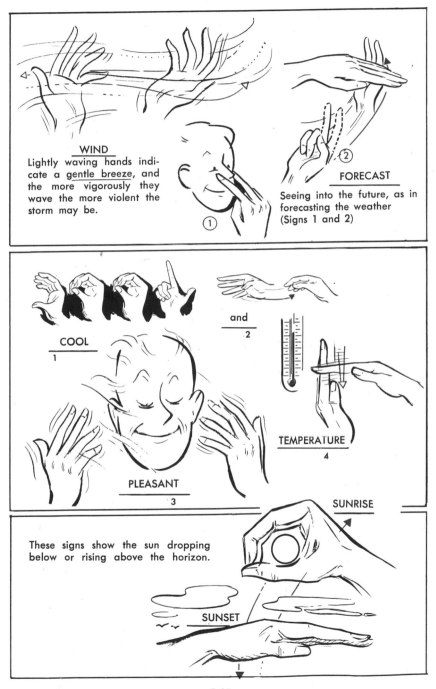

WIND

Lightly waving hands indicate a gentle breeze, and the more vigorously they wave the more violent the storm may be.

FORECAST

Seeing into the future, as in forecasting the weather (Signs 1 and 2)

COOL
1

and
2

PLEASANT
3

TEMPERATURE
4

These signs show the sun dropping below or rising above the horizon.

SUNRISE

SUNSET

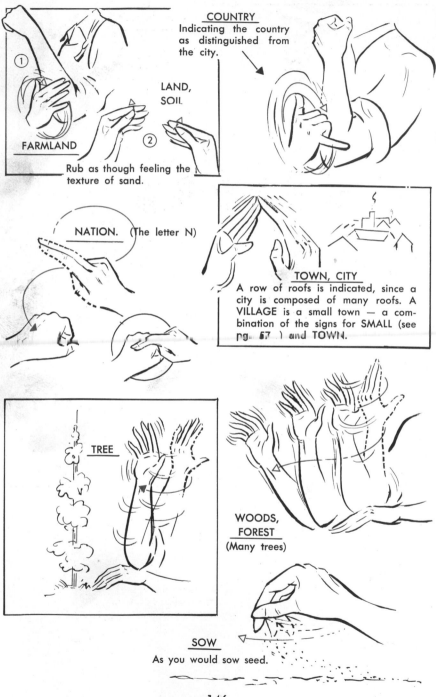

COUNTRY
Indicating the country as distinguished from the city.

FARMLAND

①

LAND, SOIL

②

Rub as though feeling the texture of sand.

NATION. (The letter N)

TOWN, CITY
A row of roofs is indicated, since a city is composed of many roofs. A VILLAGE is a small town — a combination of the signs for SMALL (see pg. 57) and TOWN.

TREE

WOODS, FOREST
(Many trees)

SOW
As you would sow seed.

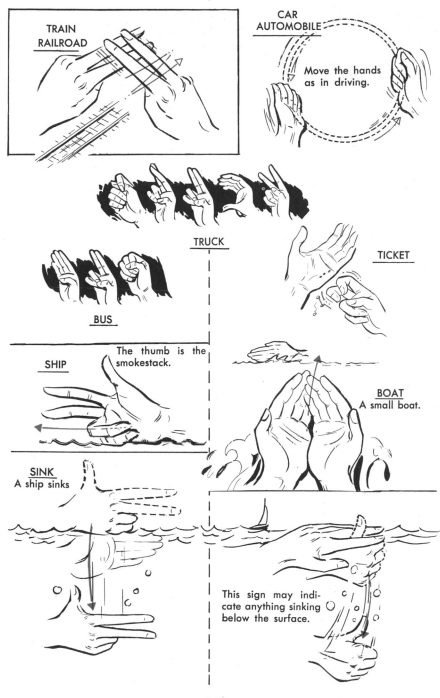

TRAIN
RAILROAD

CAR
AUTOMOBILE
Move the hands
as in driving.

TRUCK

TICKET

BUS

SHIP
The thumb is the
smokestack.

BOAT
A small boat.

SINK
A ship sinks

This sign may indi-
cate anything sinking
below the surface.

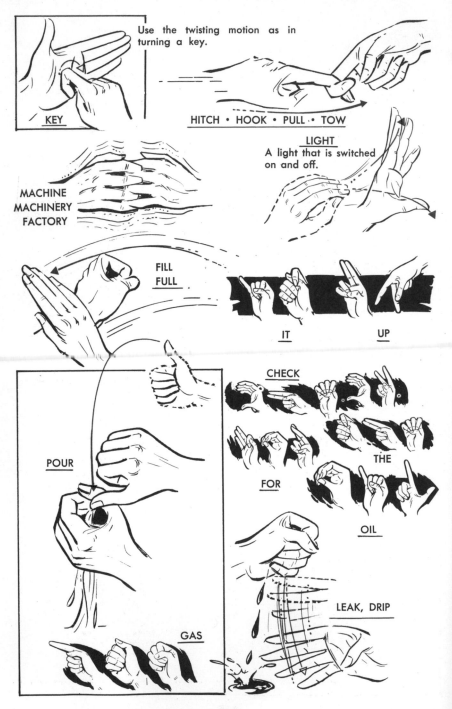

KEY

Use the twisting motion as in turning a key.

HITCH · HOOK · PULL · TOW

LIGHT
A light that is switched on and off.

MACHINE
MACHINERY
FACTORY

FILL
FULL

IT   UP

CHECK

THE

FOR

OIL

POUR

LEAK, DRIP

GAS

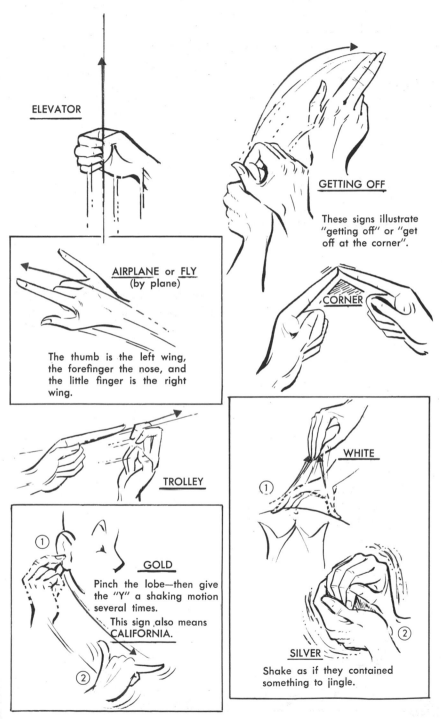

ELEVATOR

GETTING OFF

These signs illustrate "getting off" or "get off at the corner".

AIRPLANE or FLY (by plane)

The thumb is the left wing, the forefinger the nose, and the little finger is the right wing.

CORNER

TROLLEY

WHITE

①

GOLD

Pinch the lobe—then give the "Y" a shaking motion several times.

This sign also means CALIFORNIA.

②

SILVER

Shake as if they contained something to jingle.

①

②

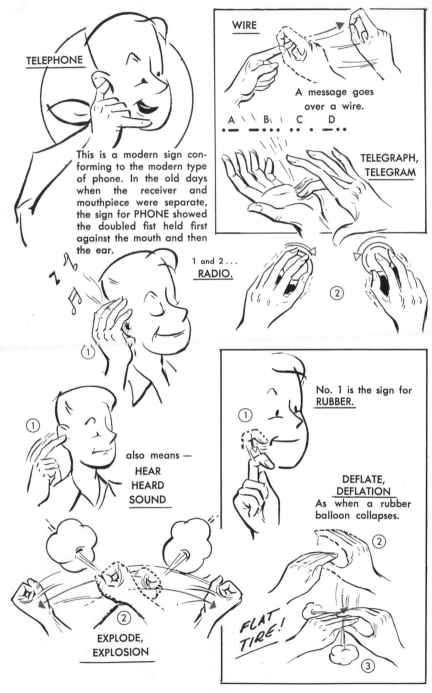

TELEPHONE

This is a modern sign conforming to the modern type of phone. In the old days when the receiver and mouthpiece were separate, the sign for PHONE showed the doubled fist held first against the mouth and then the ear.

WIRE

A message goes over a wire.

A   B   C   D

TELEGRAPH, TELEGRAM

1 and 2 ...
RADIO.

②

①

also means —
HEAR
HEARD
SOUND

No. 1 is the sign for
RUBBER.

①

DEFLATE,
DEFLATION
As when a rubber balloon collapses.

②

EXPLODE,
EXPLOSION

②

FLAT
TIRE!

③

150

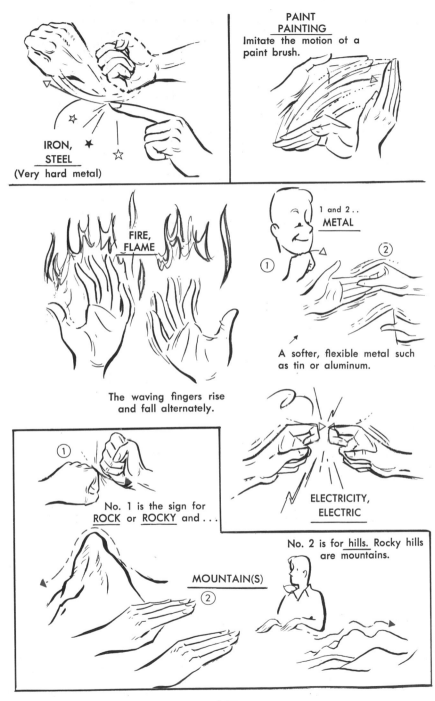

IRON, STEEL
(Very hard metal)

PAINT
PAINTING
Imitate the motion of a paint brush.

FIRE, FLAME

The waving fingers rise and fall alternately.

1 and 2..
METAL

A softer, flexible metal such as tin or aluminum.

No. 1 is the sign for ROCK or ROCKY and . . .

ELECTRICITY, ELECTRIC

No. 2 is for hills. Rocky hills are mountains.

MOUNTAIN(S)

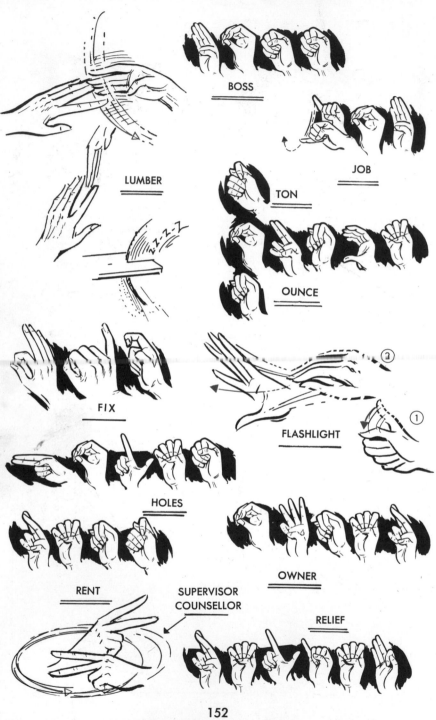

LUMBER

BOSS

JOB

TON

OUNCE

FIX

FLASHLIGHT

HOLES

OWNER

RENT

SUPERVISOR
COUNSELLOR

RELIEF

152

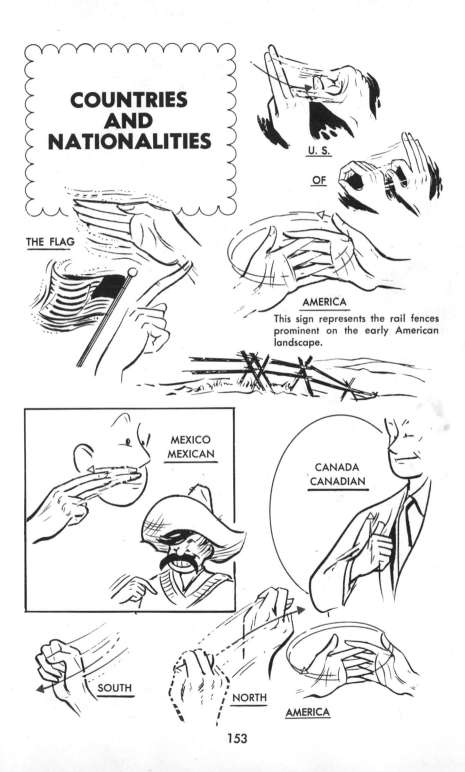

COUNTRIES AND NATIONALITIES

U. S.

OF

THE FLAG

AMERICA

This sign represents the rail fences prominent on the early American landscape.

MEXICO
MEXICAN

CANADA
CANADIAN

SOUTH

NORTH

AMERICA

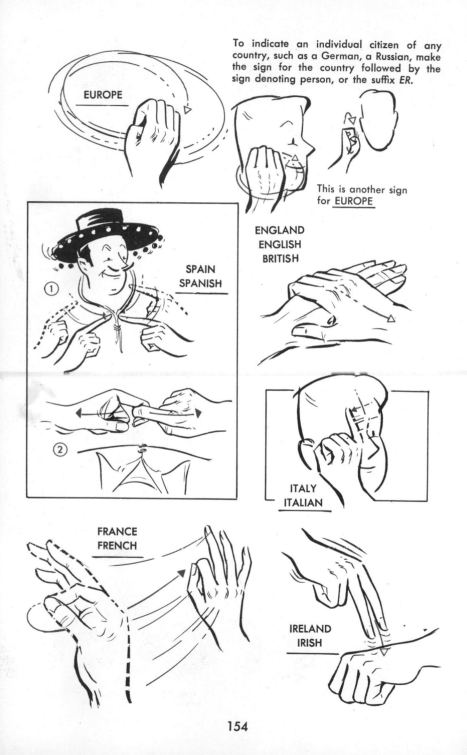

EUROPE

To indicate an individual citizen of any country, such as a German, a Russian, make the sign for the country followed by the sign denoting person, or the suffix *ER*.

This is another sign for EUROPE

SPAIN
SPANISH

① ②

ENGLAND
ENGLISH
BRITISH

ITALY
ITALIAN

FRANCE
FRENCH

IRELAND
IRISH

154

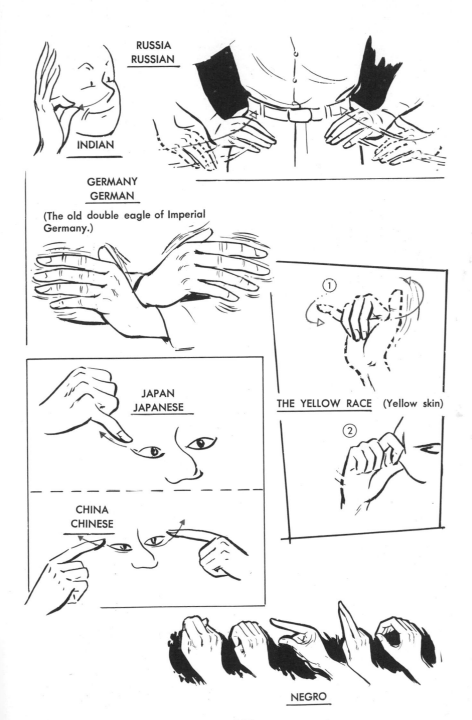

RUSSIA
RUSSIAN

INDIAN

GERMANY
GERMAN

(The old double eagle of Imperial
Germany.)

JAPAN
JAPANESE

THE YELLOW RACE   (Yellow skin)

CHINA
CHINESE

NEGRO

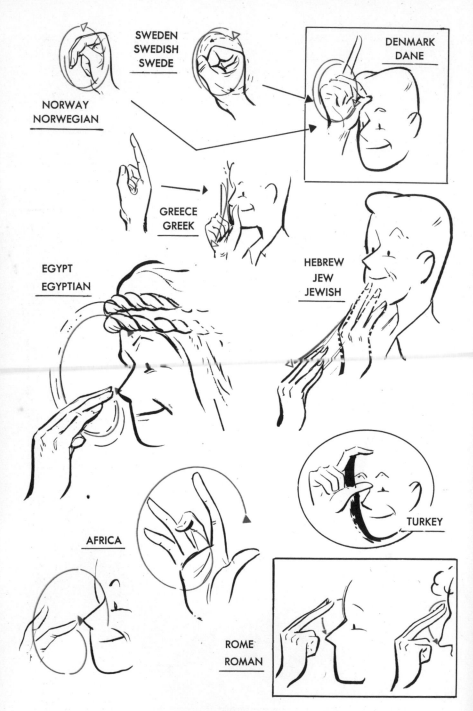

SWEDEN
SWEDISH
SWEDE

NORWAY
NORWEGIAN

DENMARK
DANE

GREECE
GREEK

EGYPT
EGYPTIAN

HEBREW
JEW
JEWISH

AFRICA

TURKEY

ROME
ROMAN

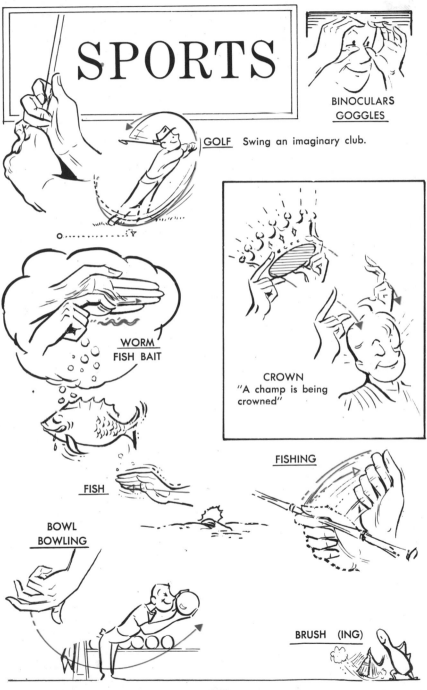

SPORTS

BINOCULARS
GOGGLES

GOLF   Swing an imaginary club.

WORM
FISH BAIT

CROWN
"A champ is being
crowned"

FISHING

FISH

BOWL
BOWLING

BRUSH   (ING)

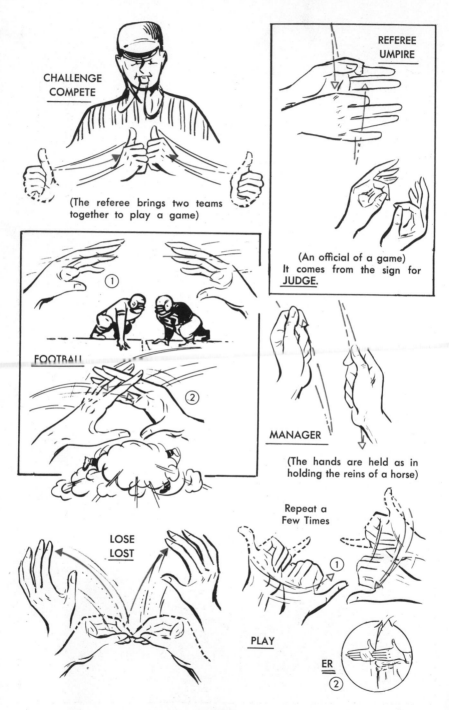

CHALLENGE
COMPETE

(The referee brings two teams together to play a game)

REFEREE
UMPIRE

(An official of a game) It comes from the sign for JUDGE.

FOOTBALL

MANAGER

(The hands are held as in holding the reins of a horse)

LOSE
LOST

Repeat a Few Times

PLAY

ER

158

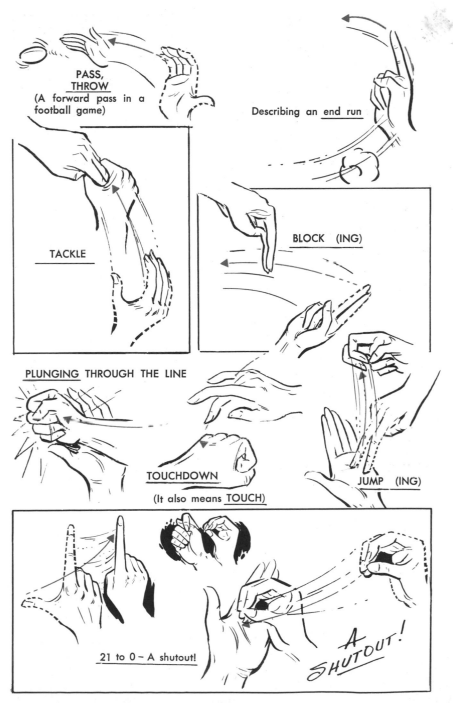

PASS,
THROW
(A forward pass in a
football game)

Describing an end run

TACKLE

BLOCK (ING)

PLUNGING THROUGH THE LINE

TOUCHDOWN

(It also means TOUCH)

JUMP (ING)

21 to 0 – A shutout!

A SHUTOUT!

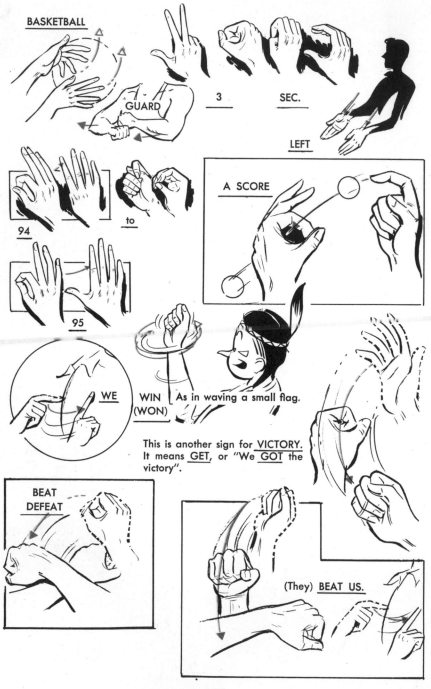

BASKETBALL

GUARD

3   SEC.

LEFT

94   to

95

A SCORE

WE   WIN   As in waving a small flag.
(WON)

This is another sign for VICTORY.
It means GET, or "We GOT the
victory".

BEAT
DEFEAT

(They) BEAT US.

160

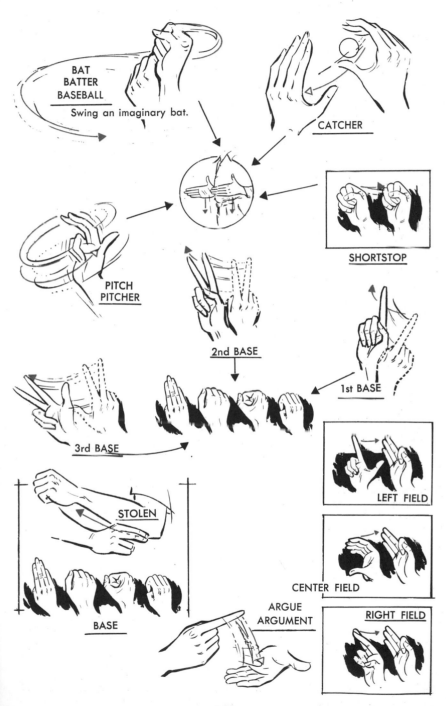

BAT
BATTER
BASEBALL
Swing an imaginary bat.

CATCHER

SHORTSTOP

PITCH
PITCHER

2nd BASE

1st BASE

3rd BASE

STOLEN

LEFT FIELD

CENTER FIELD

BASE

ARGUE
ARGUMENT

RIGHT FIELD

161

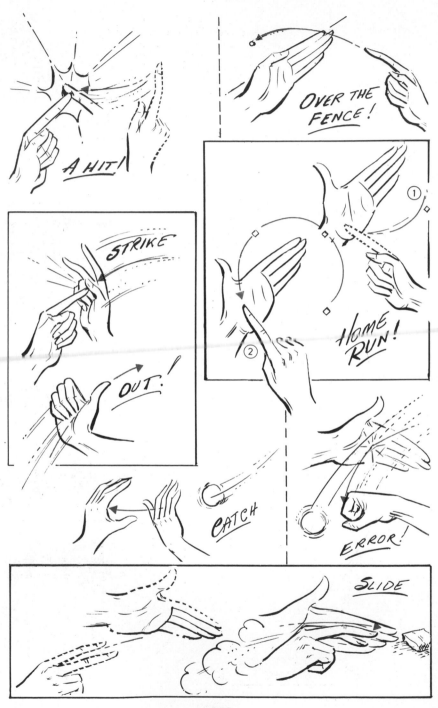

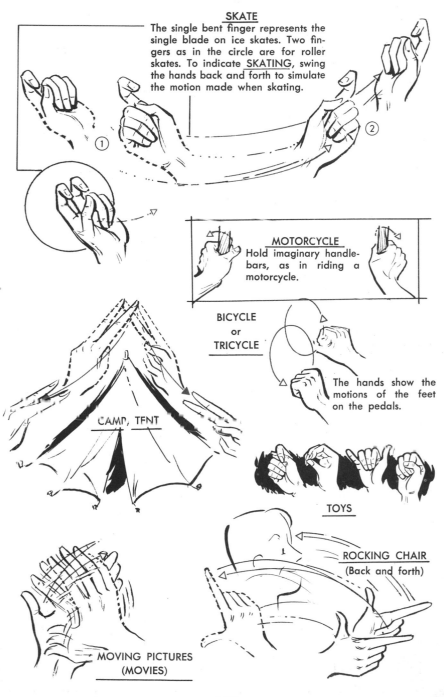

SKATE
The single bent finger represents the single blade on ice skates. Two fingers as in the circle are for roller skates. To indicate SKATING, swing the hands back and forth to simulate the motion made when skating.

① ②

MOTORCYCLE
Hold imaginary handlebars, as in riding a motorcycle.

BICYCLE
or
TRICYCLE

The hands show the motions of the feet on the pedals.

CAMP, TENT

TOYS

MOVING PICTURES
(MOVIES)

ROCKING CHAIR
(Back and forth)

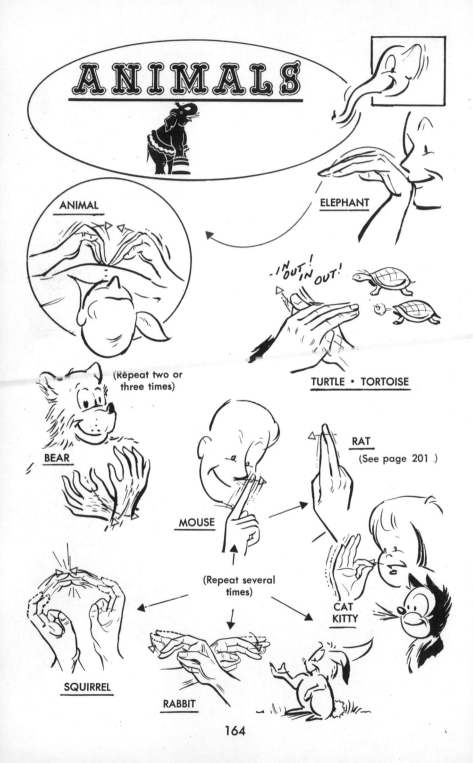

ANIMALS

ANIMAL

ELEPHANT

IN OUT! IN OUT!

TURTLE • TORTOISE

(Repeat two or three times)

BEAR

MOUSE

RAT
(See page 201.)

CAT
KITTY

(Repeat several times)

SQUIRREL

RABBIT

164

HUNTING (Shooting a gun)

1 and 2 . . .
CHICKEN

DUCK

① ②

ROOSTER

① ②

1 and 2 . . .
ROBIN

TURKEY

FOX

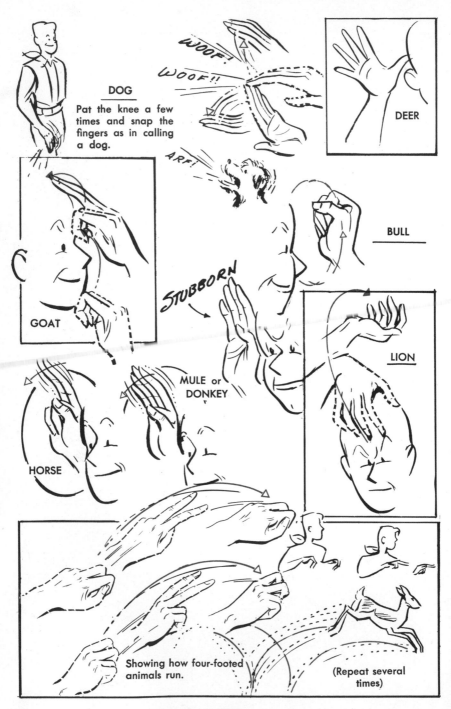

DOG

Pat the knee a few times and snap the fingers as in calling a dog.

WOOF!
WOOF!!

DEER

ARF!

BULL

GOAT

STUBBORN

MULE or DONKEY

LION

HORSE

Showing how four-footed animals run.

(Repeat several times)

166

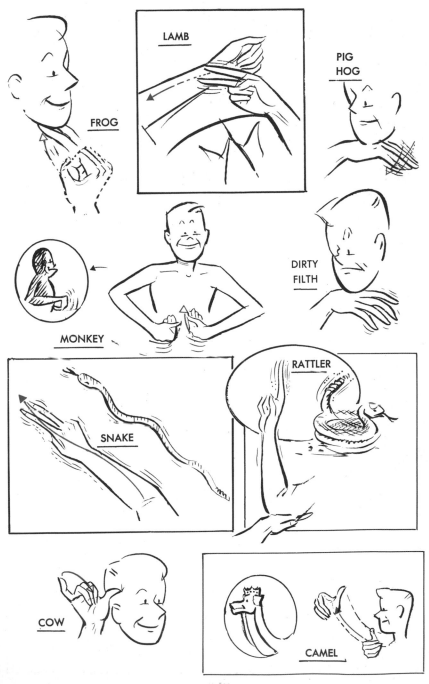

FROG

LAMB

PIG
HOG

MONKEY

DIRTY
FILTH

SNAKE

RATTLER

COW

CAMEL

167

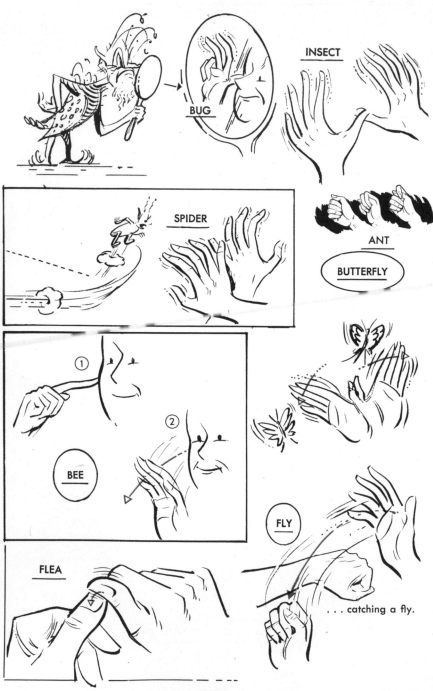

INSECT

BUG

SPIDER

ANT

BUTTERFLY

BEE

FLY

FLEA

. . . catching a fly.

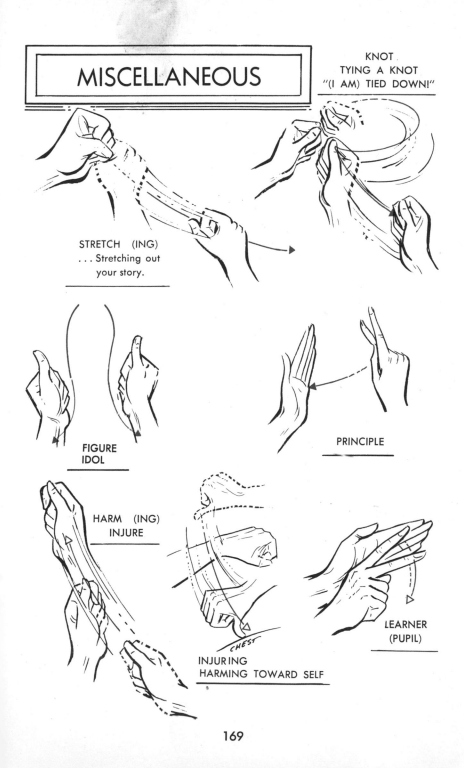

MISCELLANEOUS

KNOT
TYING A KNOT
"(I AM) TIED DOWN!"

STRETCH (ING)
... Stretching out
your story.

FIGURE
IDOL

PRINCIPLE

HARM (ING)
INJURE

INJURING
HARMING TOWARD SELF

CHEST

LEARNER
(PUPIL)

169

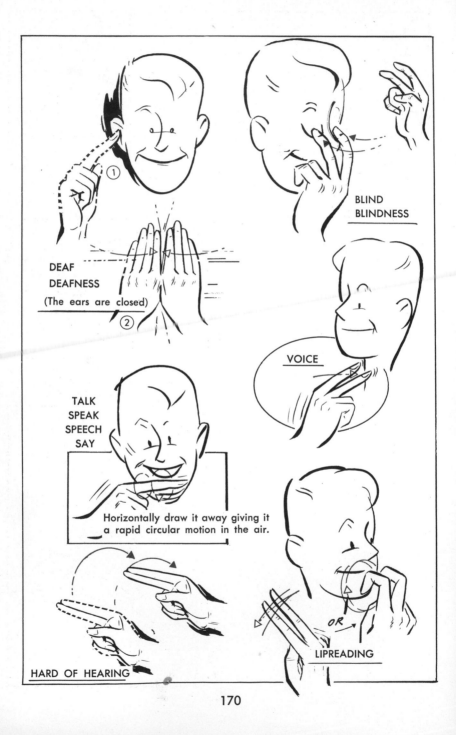

BLIND
BLINDNESS

DEAF
DEAFNESS
(The ears are closed)

VOICE

TALK
SPEAK
SPEECH
SAY

Horizontally draw it away giving it
a rapid circular motion in the air.

OR

LIPREADING

HARD OF HEARING

170

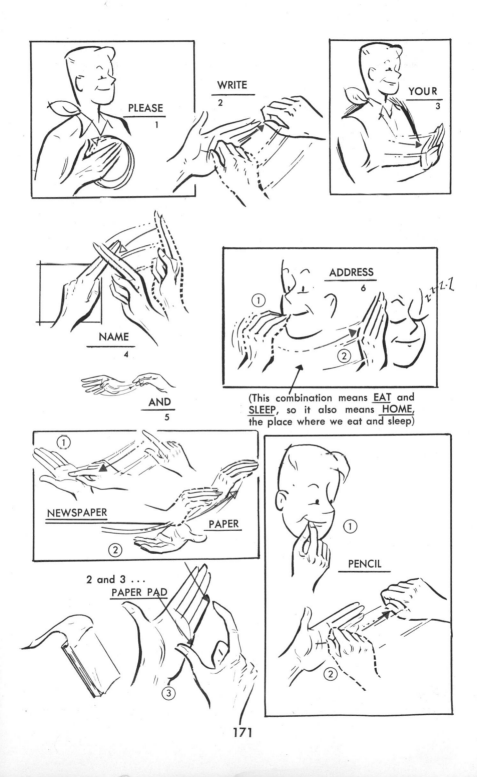

PLEASE
1

WRITE
2

YOUR
3

NAME
4

AND
5

ADDRESS
6

(This combination means EAT and SLEEP, so it also means HOME, the place where we eat and sleep)

NEWSPAPER

PAPER

2 and 3 . . .
PAPER PAD

PENCIL

171

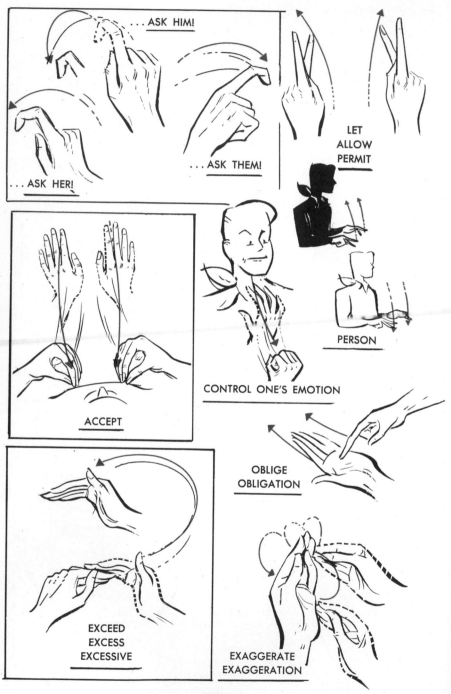

...ASK HIM!

...ASK HER!

...ASK THEM!

LET
ALLOW
PERMIT

PERSON

ACCEPT

CONTROL ONE'S EMOTION

OBLIGE
OBLIGATION

EXCEED
EXCESS
EXCESSIVE

EXAGGERATE
EXAGGERATION

YES

...No, No!

1 and 2...
CONGRATULATE
CONGRATULATION
PRAISE
COMMEND

① ②

INDECISION
UNCERTAIN
"On the fence"

CLEVER

DUTY

FATHER   MOTHER

In common usage we do not bother to make the complete signs for MOTHER and FATHER. We merely make the first sign with the thumb at the forehead with fingers extended (FATHER) or at the chin (MOTHER).

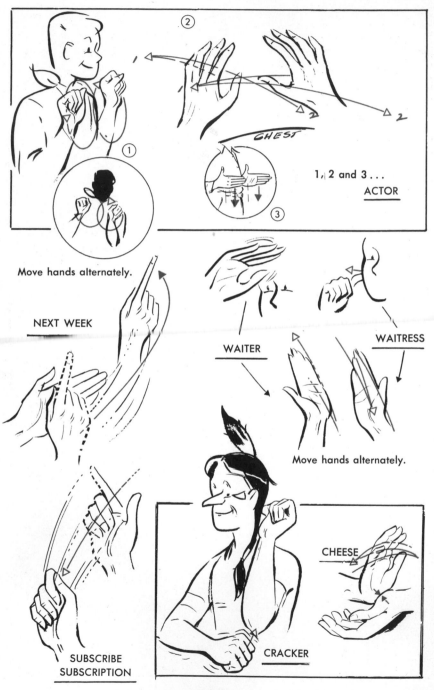

② ①

CHEST

③

1, 2 and 3 . . .
ACTOR

Move hands alternately.

NEXT WEEK

WAITER

WAITRESS

Move hands alternately.

CHEESE

SUBSCRIBE
SUBSCRIPTION

CRACKER

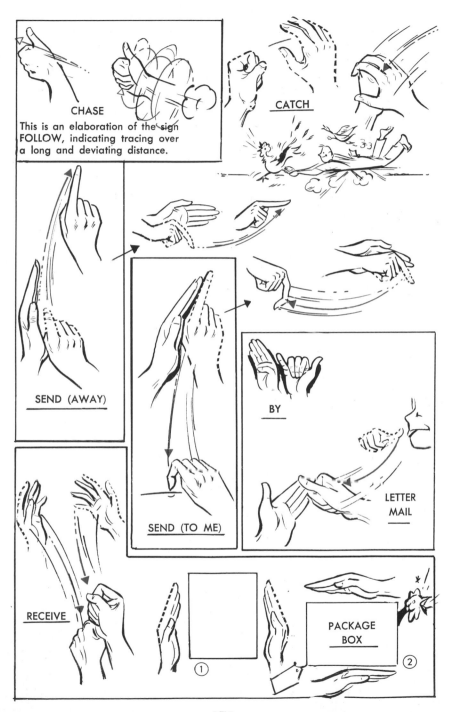

CHASE
This is an elaboration of the sign FOLLOW, indicating tracing over a long and deviating distance.

CATCH

SEND (AWAY)

SEND (TO ME)

BY

LETTER
MAIL

RECEIVE

① PACKAGE
BOX ②

175

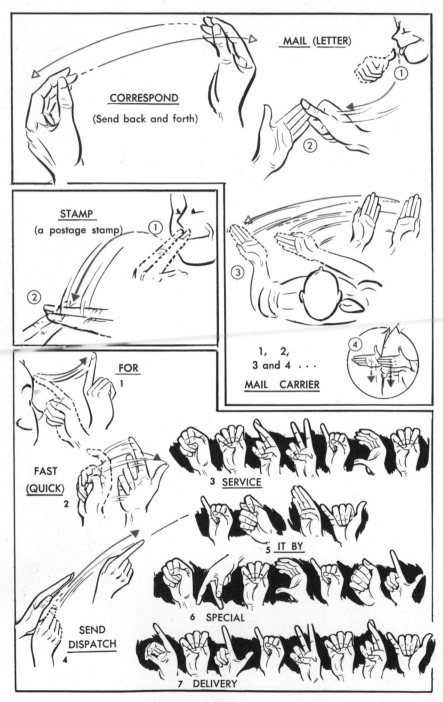

MAIL (LETTER)

CORRESPOND
(Send back and forth)

STAMP
(a postage stamp)

1, 2,
3 and 4 . . .
MAIL CARRIER

FOR
1

FAST
(QUICK)
2

3 SERVICE

5 IT BY

6 SPECIAL

SEND
DISPATCH
4

7 DELIVERY

176

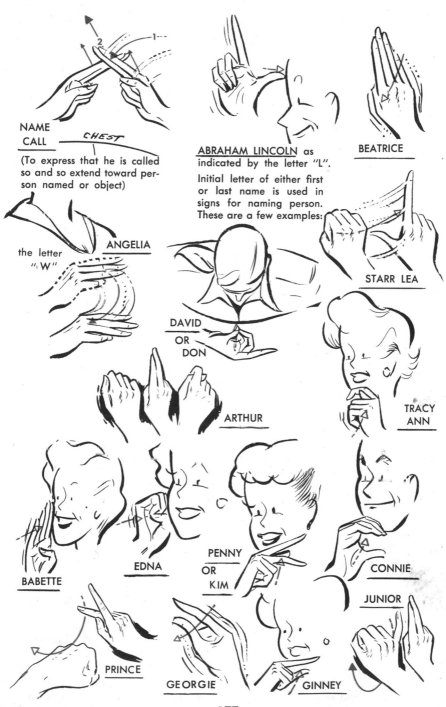

NAME CALL — _CHEST_

(To express that he is called so and so extend toward person named or object)

the letter "W"

ANGELIA

ABRAHAM LINCOLN as indicated by the letter "L".

Initial letter of either first or last name is used in signs for naming person. These are a few examples:

BEATRICE

STARR LEA

DAVID OR DON

ARTHUR

TRACY ANN

BABETTE

EDNA

PENNY OR KIM

CONNIE

JUNIOR

PRINCE

GEORGIE

GINNEY

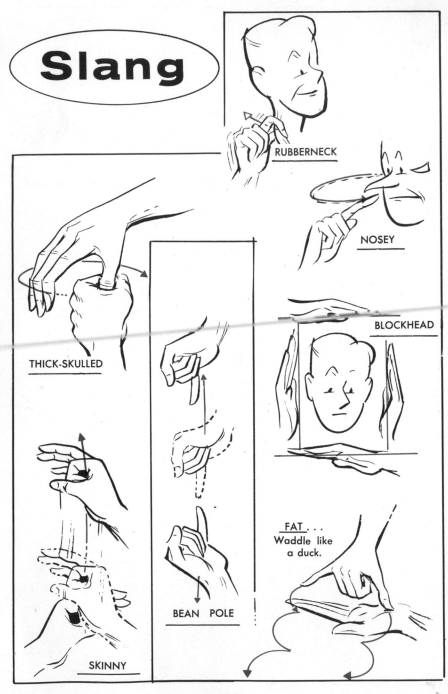

Slang

RUBBERNECK

NOSEY

THICK-SKULLED

BLOCKHEAD

SKINNY

BEAN POLE

FAT . . .
Waddle like
a duck.

178

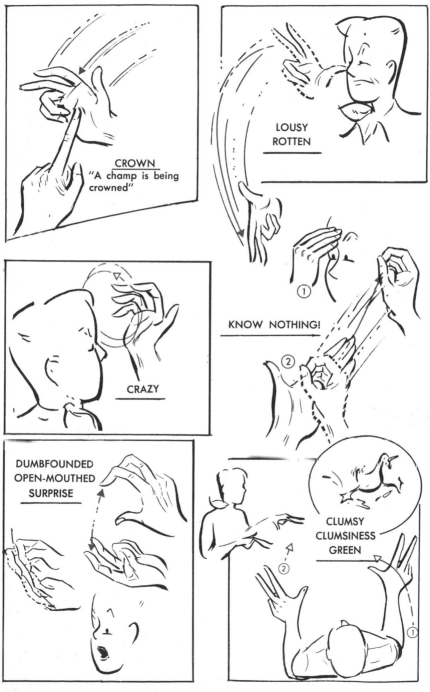

CROWN
"A champ is being crowned"

LOUSY
ROTTEN

CRAZY

KNOW NOTHING!

DUMBFOUNDED
OPEN-MOUTHED
SURPRISE

CLUMSY
CLUMSINESS
GREEN

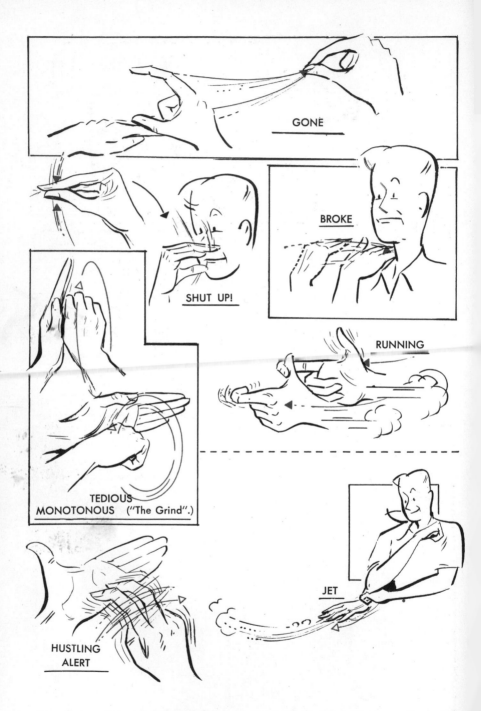

GONE

BROKE

SHUT UP!

RUNNING

TEDIOUS
MONOTONOUS ("The Grind".)

JET

HUSTLING
ALERT

180

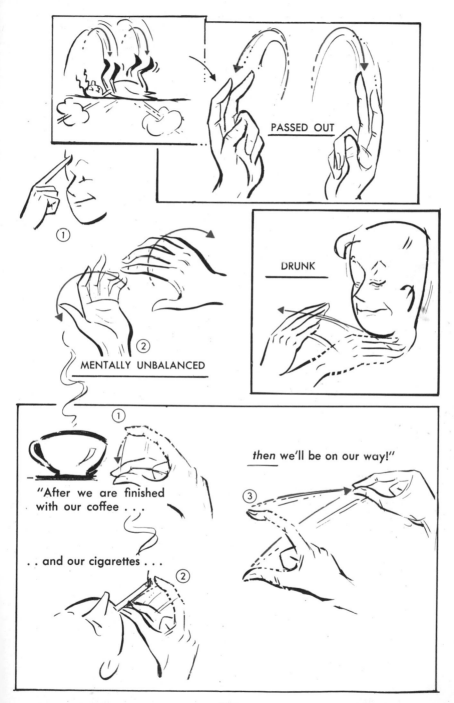

PASSED OUT

DRUNK

MENTALLY UNBALANCED

"After we are finished with our coffee . . .

.. and our cigarettes . . .

then we'll be on our way!"

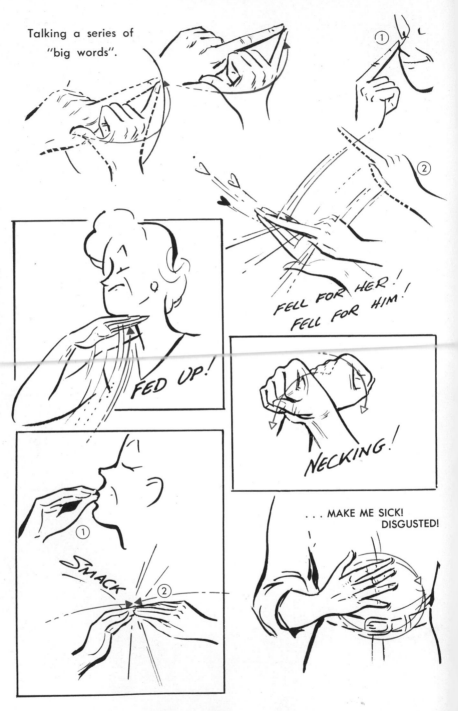

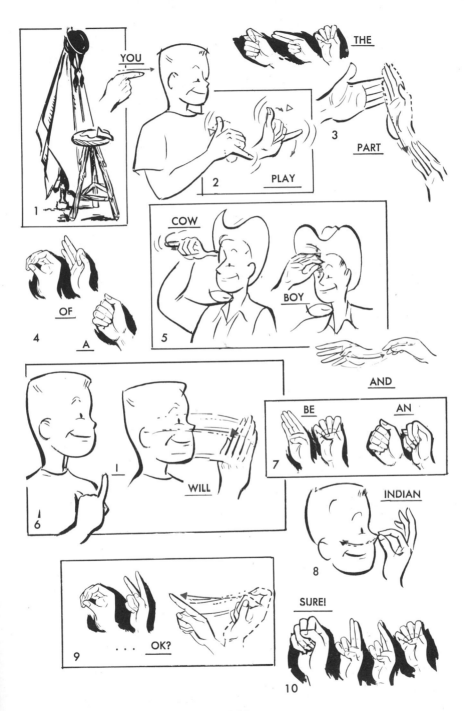

YOU

THE

2 PLAY

3

PART

4 OF A

5 COW BOY

AND

6 I WILL

7 BE AN

8 INDIAN

9 ... OK?

SURE!

10

183

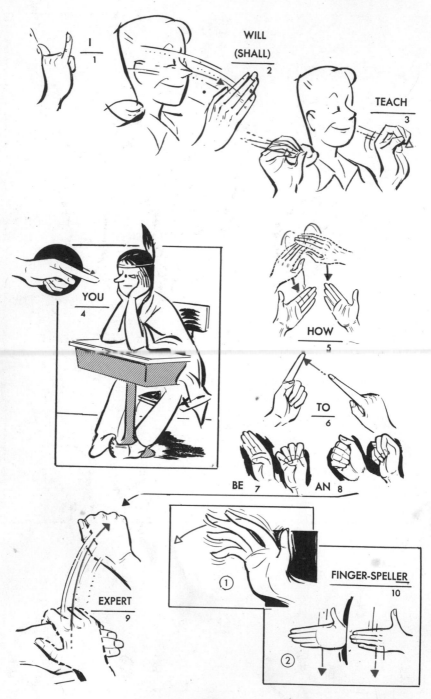

I
1

WILL
(SHALL)
2

TEACH
3

YOU
4

HOW
5

TO
6

BE 7

AN 8

EXPERT
9

①

FINGER-SPELLER
10

②

184

The AMERICAN MANUAL ALPHABET
(FINGERSPELLING)

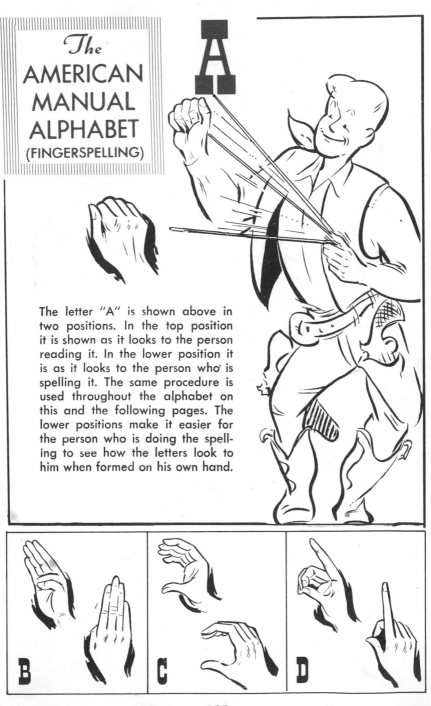

The letter "A" is shown above in two positions. In the top position it is shown as it looks to the person reading it. In the lower position it is as it looks to the person who is spelling it. The same procedure is used throughout the alphabet on this and the following pages. The lower positions make it easier for the person who is doing the spelling to see how the letters look to him when formed on his own hand.

B

C

D

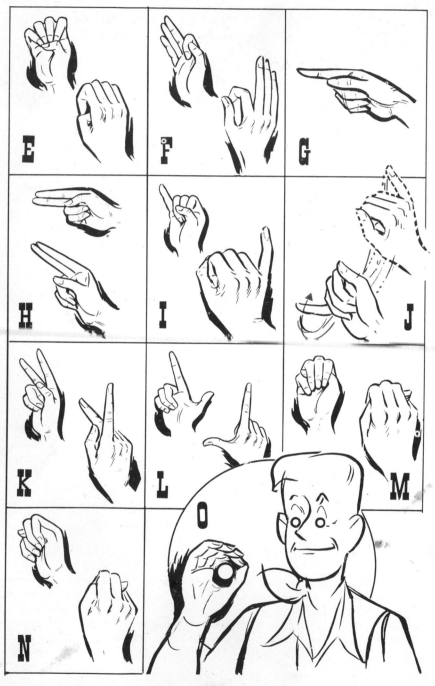

Watch D and F. The Beginner invariably confuses them.

Note that G and Q are the same, except that for Q the thumb and finger points downward.

Also, K and P are similar, but P points downward.

OH, I SEE!

Beginners confuse R, S, and T. Learn them well!

Always spell with the palm of your hand *toward* the person you are spelling to. Learn to form the letters with the fingers *only*. Do not bend the wrist. No noticeable pause or stop is made between letters or words. With practice, you learn to distinguish between words without spaces between them.

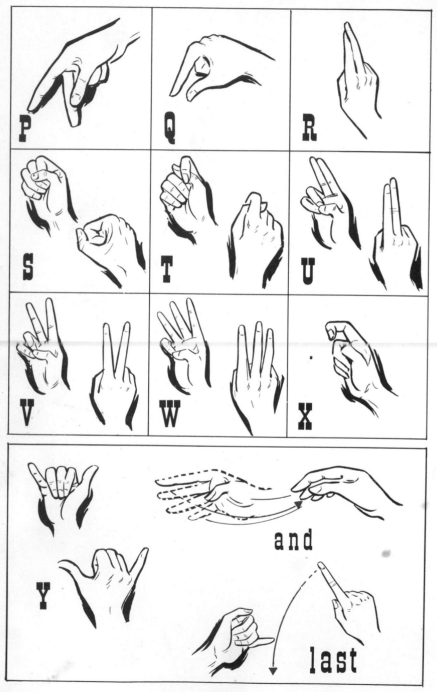

P

Q

R

S

T

U

V

W

X

Y

and

last

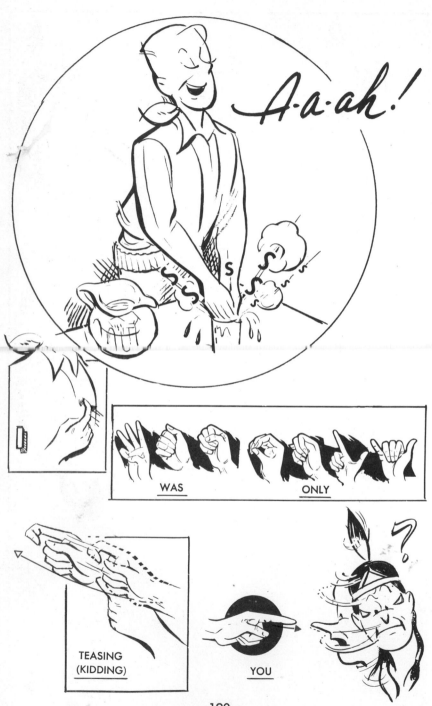

WAS

ONLY

TEASING
(KIDDING)

YOU

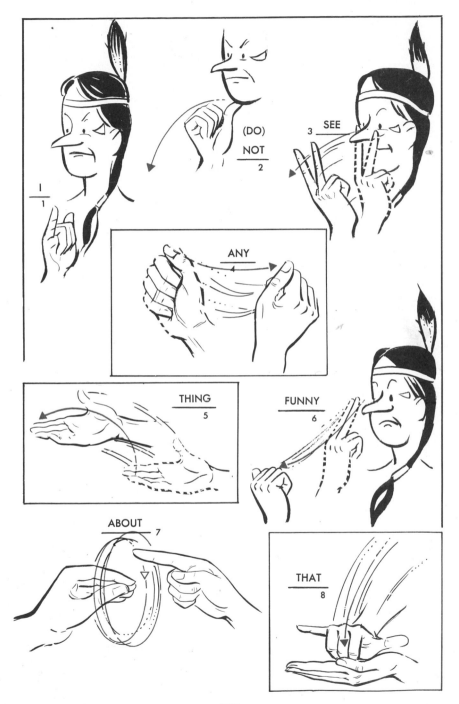

(DO)
NOT
2

SEE
3

1
1

ANY
4

THING
5

FUNNY
6

ABOUT
7

THAT
8

191

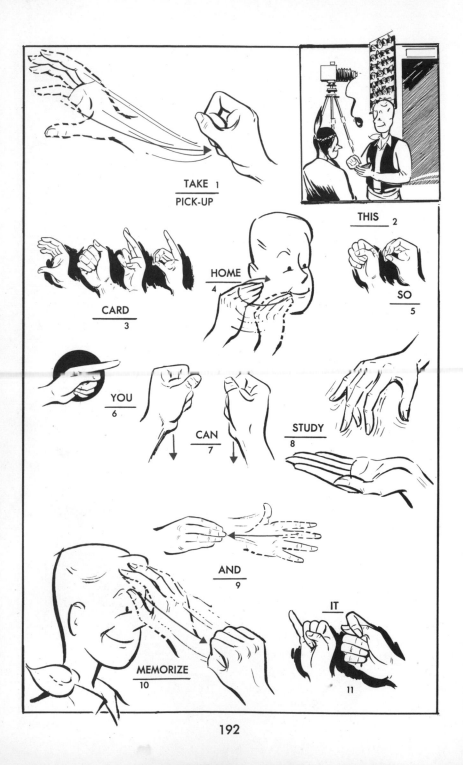

TAKE 1
PICK-UP

THIS 2

CARD 3

HOME 4

SO 5

YOU 6

CAN 7

STUDY 8

AND 9

MEMORIZE 10

IT 11

192

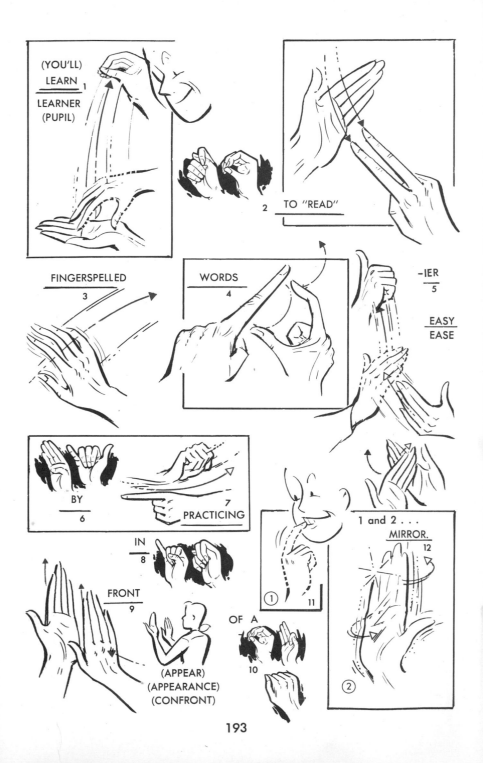

(YOU'LL)
LEARN 1
LEARNER
(PUPIL)

TO "READ"
2

FINGERSPELLED
3

WORDS
4

-IER
5

EASY
EASE

BY
6

PRACTICING
7

IN
8

FRONT
9

(APPEAR)
(APPEARANCE)
(CONFRONT)

OF A
10

1
11

1 and 2 . . .
MIRROR.
12

2

193

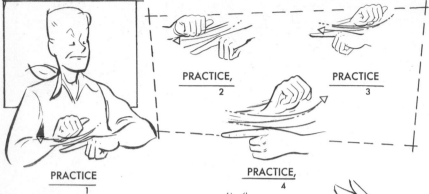

PRACTICE, 2

PRACTICE 3

PRACTICE 1

PRACTICE, 4

AS 5

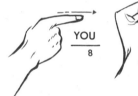

MUCH 6

AS 7

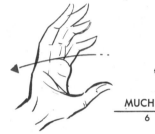

YOU 8

CAN 9

I 1

WILL (SHALL) 2

The letters T

TRY 3

194

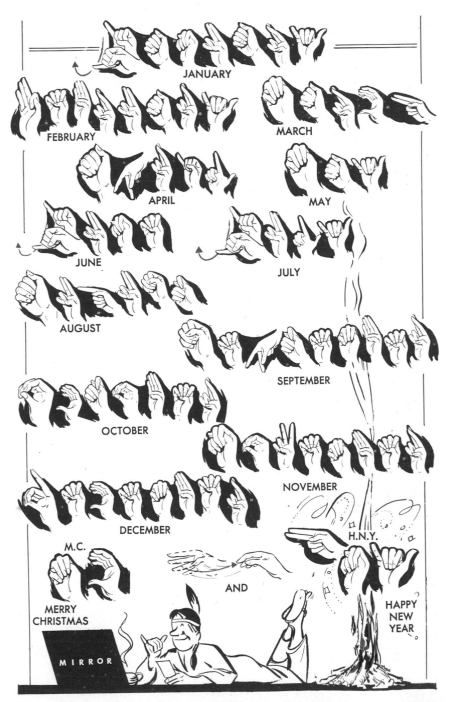

JANUARY

FEBRUARY

MARCH

APRIL

MAY

JUNE

JULY

AUGUST

SEPTEMBER

OCTOBER

NOVEMBER

DECEMBER

H.N.Y.

M.C.

AND

MERRY
CHRISTMAS

MIRROR

HAPPY
NEW
YEAR

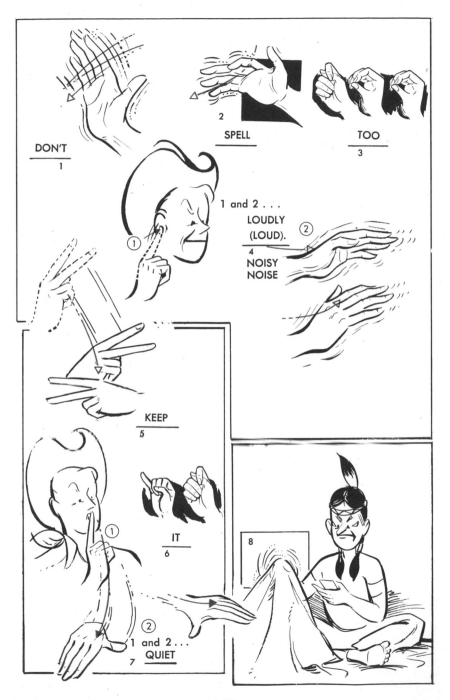

DON'T
1

SPELL
2

TOO
3

1 and 2 . . .
LOUDLY
(LOUD).
4
NOISY
NOISE

KEEP
5

IT
6

1 and 2 . . .
QUIET
7

197

198

TROUBLE?

QUESTION

Draw a question mark in the air with the "D" hand

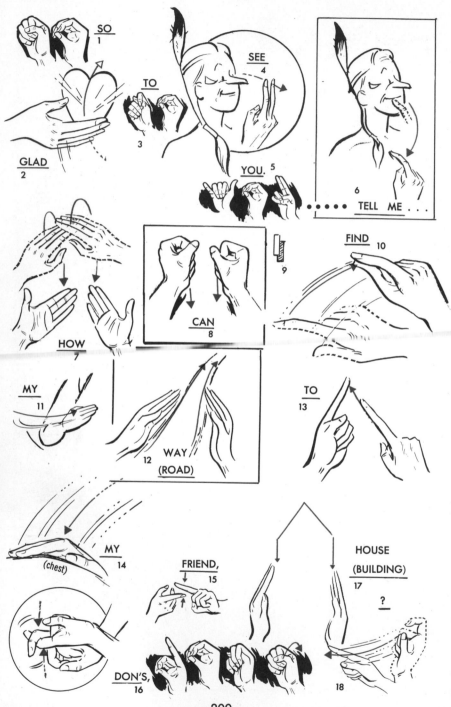

SO
1

GLAD
2

TO
3

SEE
4

YOU.
5

6
• • • • • TELL ME . . .

HOW
7

CAN
8

9

FIND
10

MY
11

WAY
(ROAD)
12

TO
13

MY
14
(chest)

FRIEND,
15

HOUSE
(BUILDING)
17

?

DON'S,
16

18

200

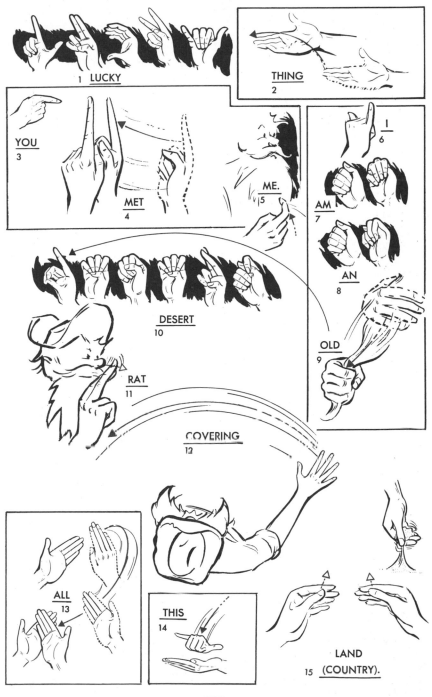

1 LUCKY

THING
2

YOU
3

MET
4

ME.
5

I
6

AM
7

AN
8

OLD
9

DESERT
10

RAT
11

COVERING
12

ALL
13

THIS
14

LAND
15 (COUNTRY).

201

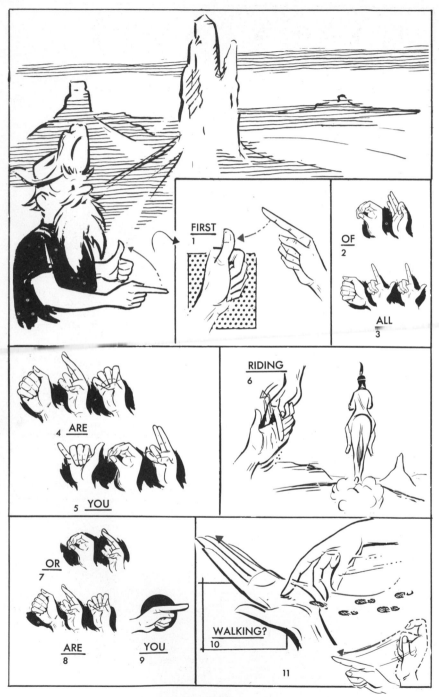

FIRST
1

OF
2

ALL
3

4 ARE

5 YOU

RIDING
6

OR
7

ARE
8

YOU
9

WALKING?
10

11

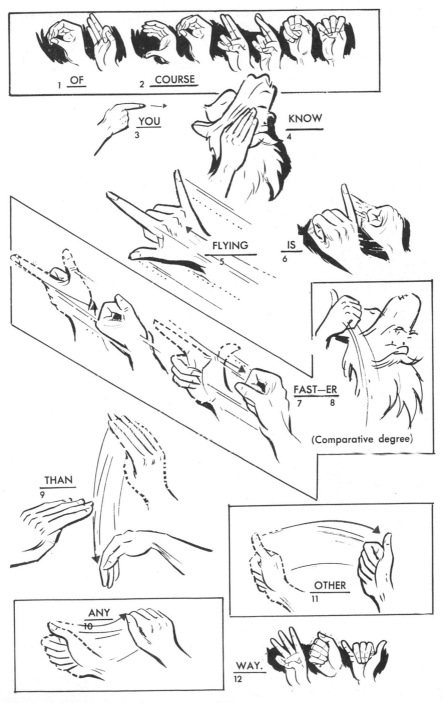

1 OF 2 COURSE 3 YOU 4 KNOW 5 FLYING 6 IS 7 FAST—ER 8

(Comparative degree)

9 THAN 10 ANY 11 OTHER 12 WAY.

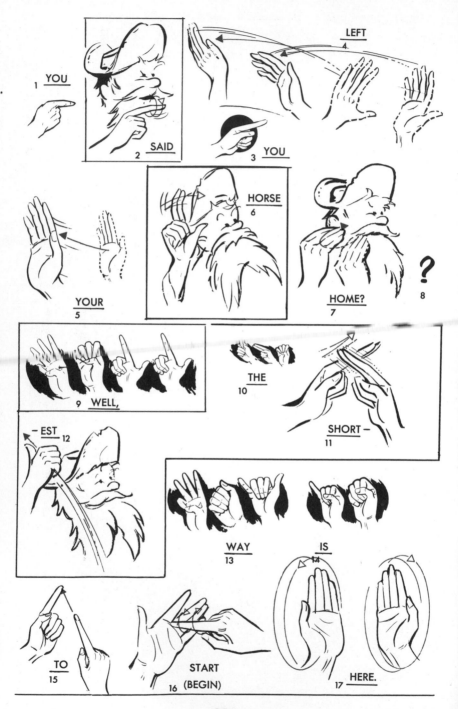

1 YOU 2 SAID 3 YOU 4 LEFT 5 YOUR 6 HORSE 7 HOME? 8 ? 9 WELL, 10 THE 11 SHORT – 12 – EST 13 WAY 14 IS 15 TO 16 START (BEGIN) 17 HERE.

204

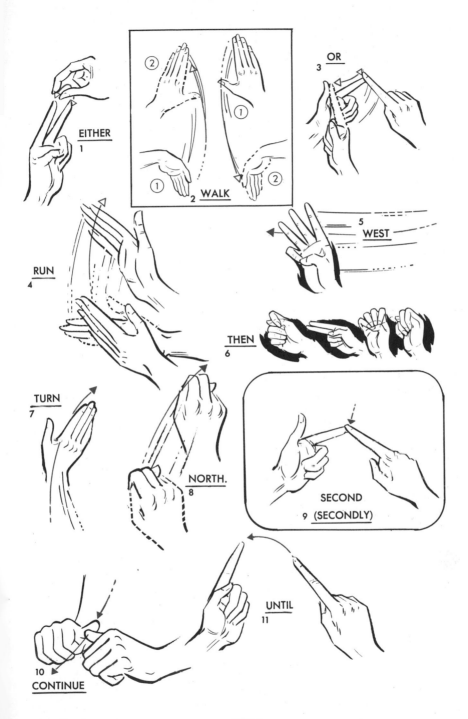

EITHER
1

2

1

1

2

WALK

OR
3

RUN
4

WEST
5

THEN
6

TURN
7

NORTH.
8

SECOND
9 (SECONDLY)

CONTINUE
10

UNTIL
11

205

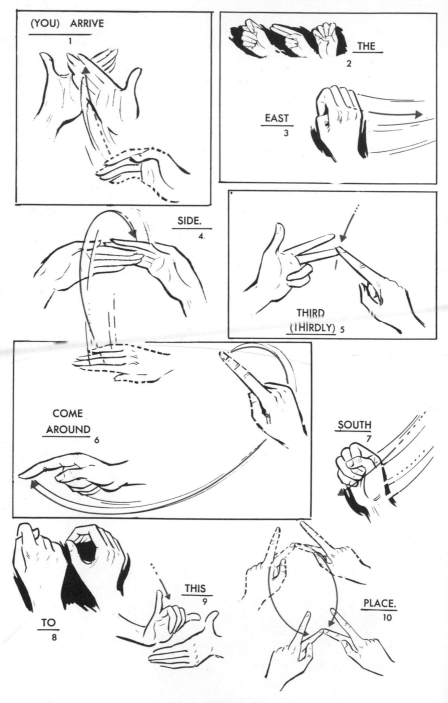

(YOU) ARRIVE
1

THE
2

EAST
3

SIDE.
4.

THIRD
(THIRDLY) 5

COME
AROUND
6

SOUTH
7

TO
8

THIS
9

PLACE.
10

206

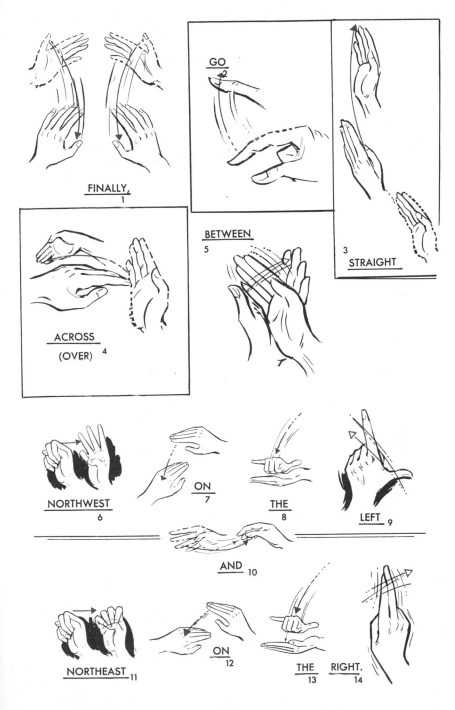

FINALLY,
1

GO
2

STRAIGHT
3

ACROSS
(OVER) 4

BETWEEN
5

NORTHWEST
6

ON
7

THE
8

LEFT 9

AND 10

NORTHEAST 11

ON
12

THE
13

RIGHT.
14

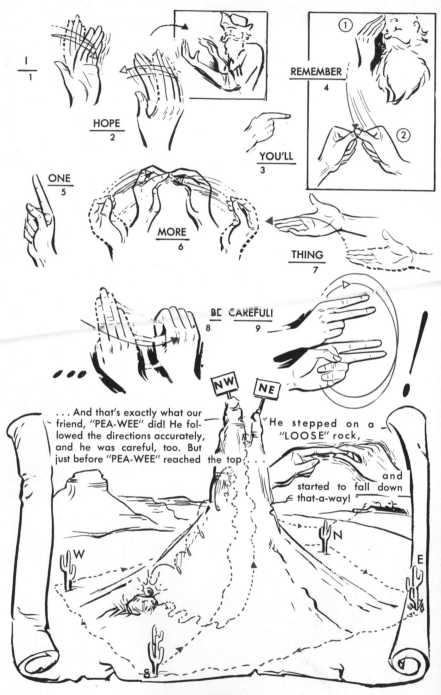

$\dfrac{1}{1}$

HOPE
2

REMEMBER
4

YOU'LL
3

ONE
5

MORE
6

THING
7

BE CAREFUL!
8   9

... And that's exactly what our friend, "PEA-WEE" did! He followed the directions accurately, and he was careful, too. But just before "PEA-WEE" reached the top ...

He stepped on a "LOOSE" rock,

and started to fall down that-a-way!

NW   NE

W

N

S

E

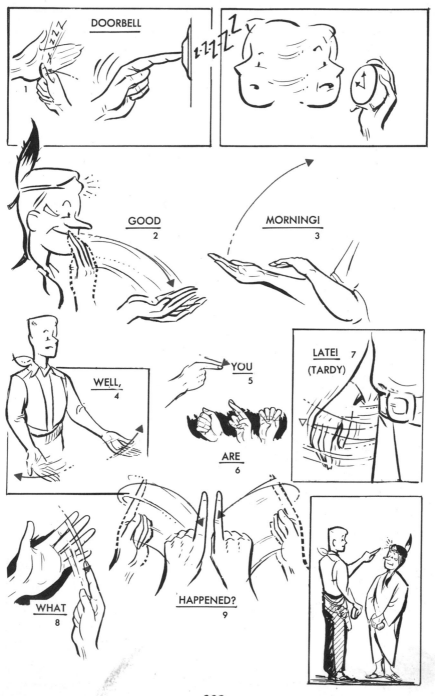

DOORBELL

GOOD
2

MORNING!
3

WELL,
4

YOU
5

ARE
6

LATE! 7
(TARDY)

WHAT
8

HAPPENED?
9

209

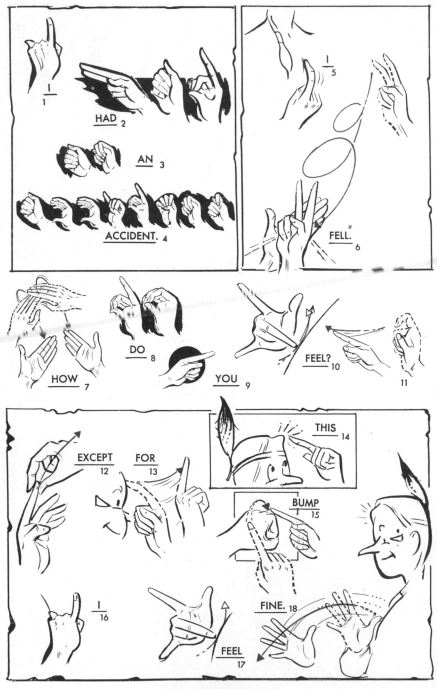

I 1

HAD 2

AN 3

ACCIDENT. 4

I 5

FELL. 6

HOW 7

DO 8

YOU 9

FEEL? 10

11

EXCEPT 12

FOR 13

THIS 14

BUMP 15

I 16

FEEL 17

FINE. 18

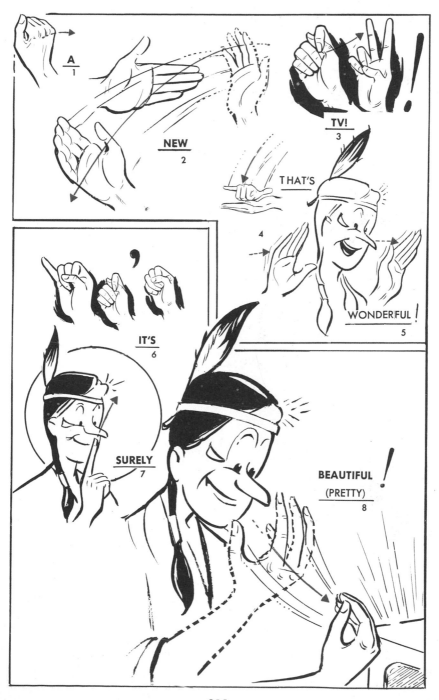

A
1

NEW
2

TV!
3

THAT'S
4

WONDERFUL!
5

IT'S
6

SURELY
7

BEAUTIFUL!
(PRETTY)
8

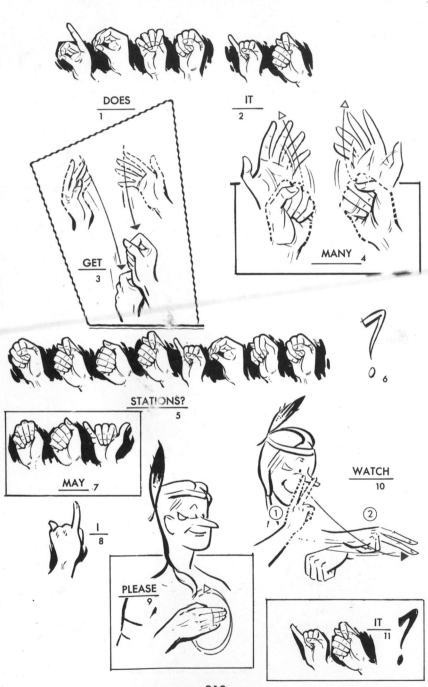

DOES
1

IT
2

GET
3

MANY
4

STATIONS?
5

0
6

MAY
7

I
8

PLEASE
9

WATCH
10

1   2

IT
11

212

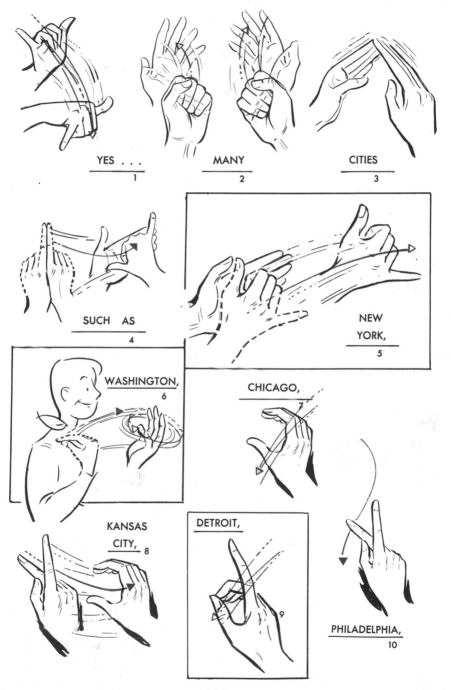

YES . . .
1

MANY
2

CITIES
3

SUCH AS
4

NEW
YORK,
5

WASHINGTON,
6

CHICAGO,
7

KANSAS
CITY, 8

DETROIT,
9

PHILADELPHIA,
10

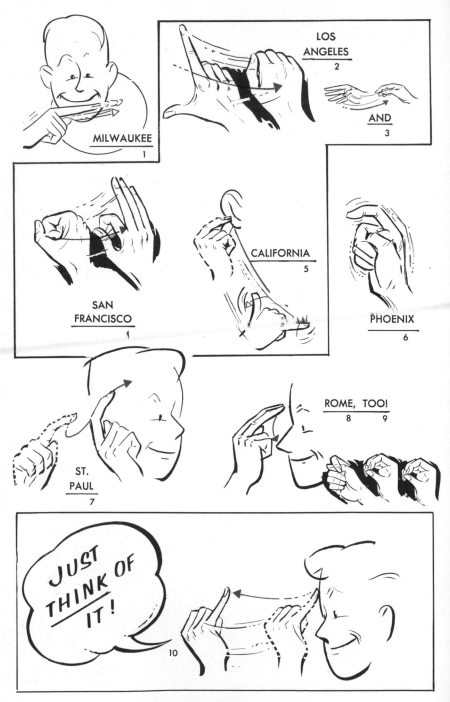

214

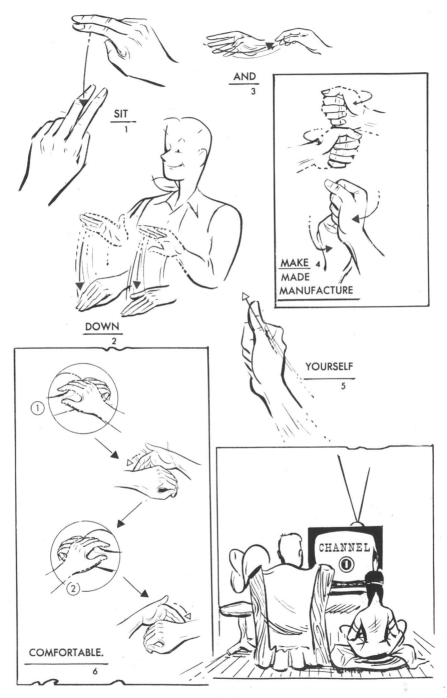

SIT
1

AND
3

DOWN
2

MAKE 4
MADE
MANUFACTURE

YOURSELF
5

① ②

COMFORTABLE.
6

CHANNEL

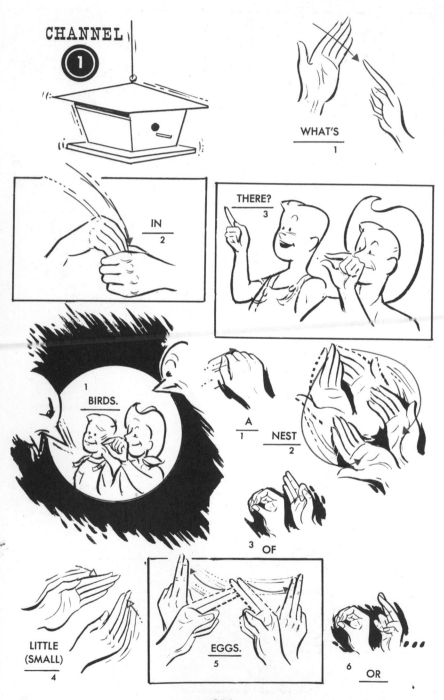

CHANNEL **1**

WHAT'S
1

IN
2

THERE?
3

BIRDS.
1

A
1

NEST
2

OF
3

LITTLE
(SMALL)
4

EGGS.
5

OR
6

216

217

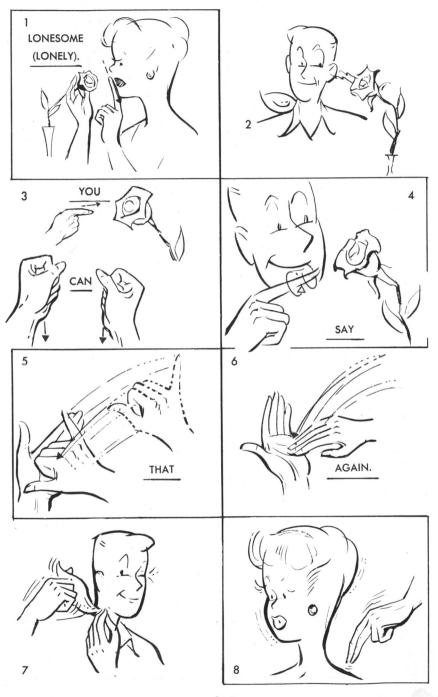

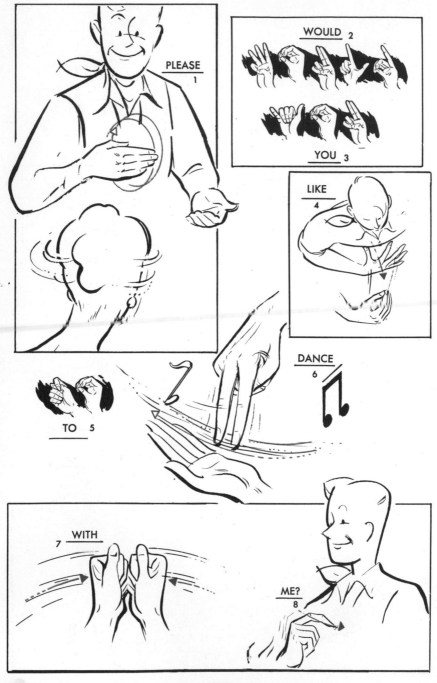

PLEASE
1

WOULD 2

YOU 3

LIKE
4

DANCE
6

TO 5

WITH
7

ME?
8

220

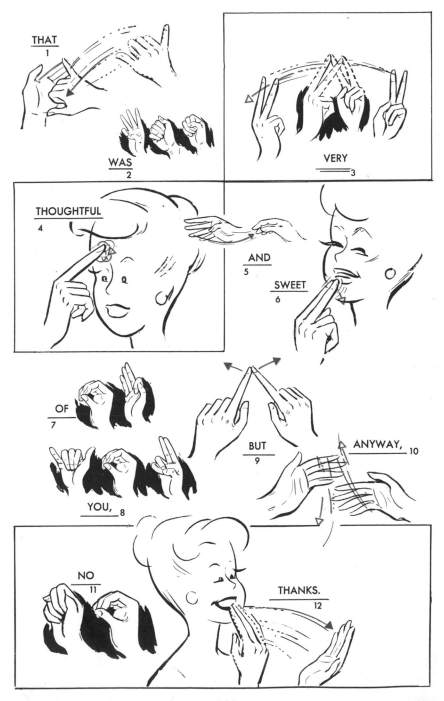

THAT
1

WAS
2

VERY
3

THOUGHTFUL
4

AND
5

SWEET
6

OF
7

YOU,
8

BUT
9

ANYWAY,
10

NO
11

THANKS.
12

221

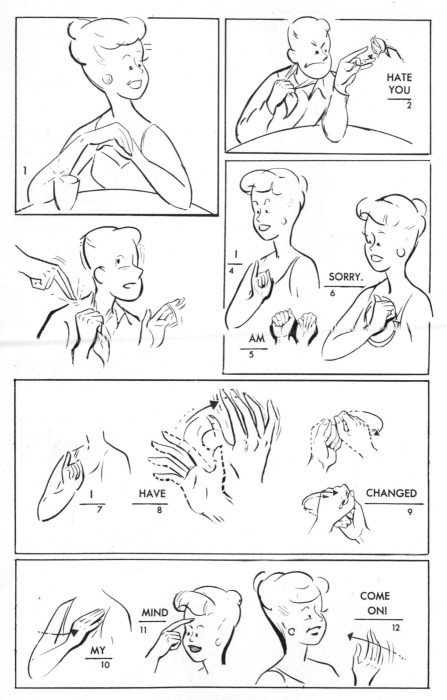

I

ENJOYED
2

THAT
3

PROGRAM.
4

HOW
5

DID
6

YOU
7

LIKE
8

IT
9

YOURSELF?
10

11

223

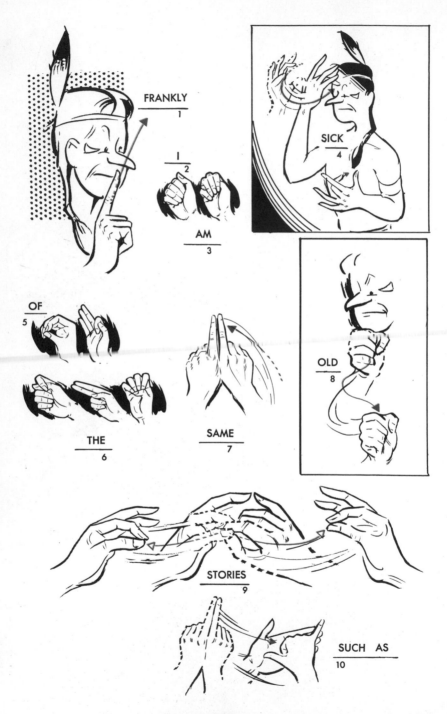

FRANKLY
1

I
2

AM
3

SICK
4

OF
5

THE
6

SAME
7

OLD
8

STORIES
9

SUCH AS
10

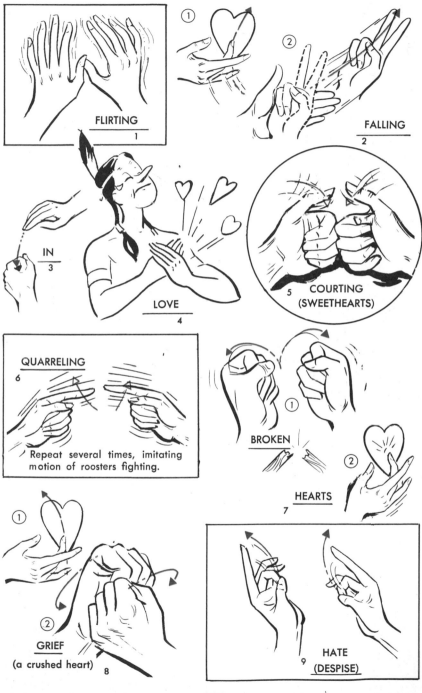

FLIRTING
1

① ②

FALLING
2

IN
3

LOVE
4

COURTING
5 (SWEETHEARTS)

QUARRELING
6

Repeat several times, imitating motion of roosters fighting.

BROKEN

①
②

HEARTS
7

①

②

GRIEF
(a crushed heart)
8

HATE
9 (DESPISE)

225

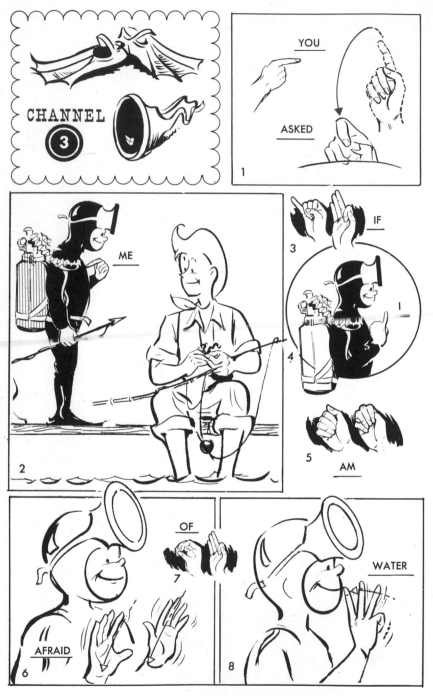

CHANNEL ③

1 YOU ASKED

2 ME

3 IF

4 I

5 AM

6 AFRAID

7 OF

8 WATER

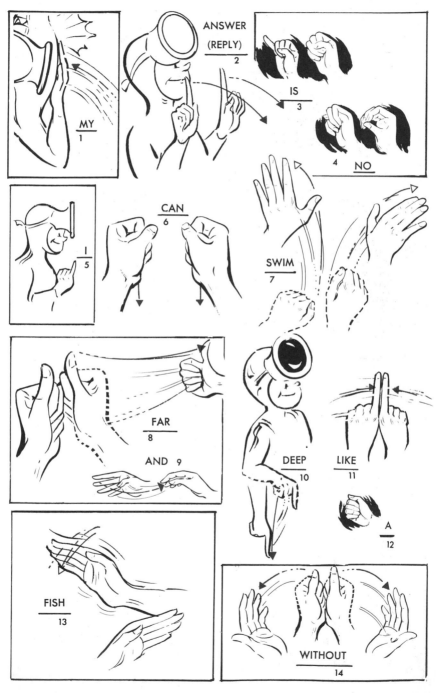

MY
1

ANSWER
(REPLY)
2

IS
3

NO
4

I
5

CAN
6

SWIM
7

FAR
8

AND 9

DEEP
10

LIKE
11

A
12

FISH
13

WITHOUT
14

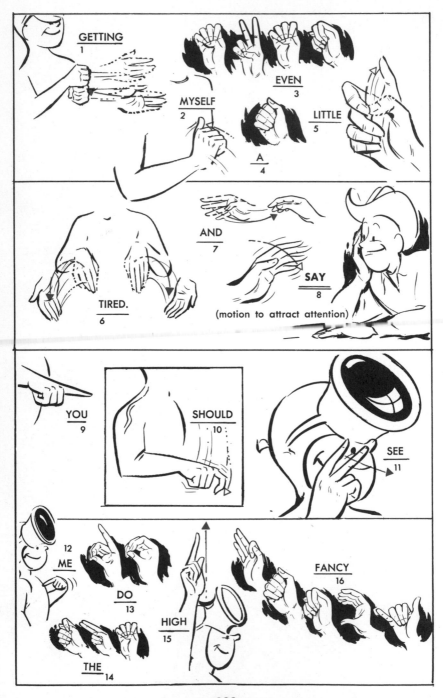

GETTING
1

MYSELF
2

EVEN
3

A
4

LITTLE
5

TIRED.
6

AND
7

SAY
8

(motion to attract attention)

YOU
9

SHOULD
10

SEE
11

ME
12

DO
13

THE
14

HIGH
15

FANCY
16

228

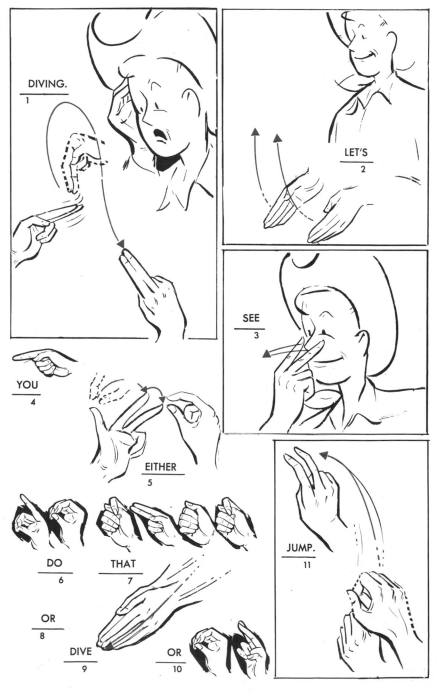

DIVING.
1

LET'S
2

SEE
3

YOU
4

EITHER
5

DO
6

THAT
7

OR
8

DIVE
9

OR
10

JUMP.
11

2

WHAT'S
3

WRONG?
(MISTAKE)
4

1
1

.BECAME
2

WET!
(DAMP)
3

231

IDEA!

TV

HAVE
2

1

NEVER
3

SEEN
4

SO
5

WATER
7

6 MUCH

232

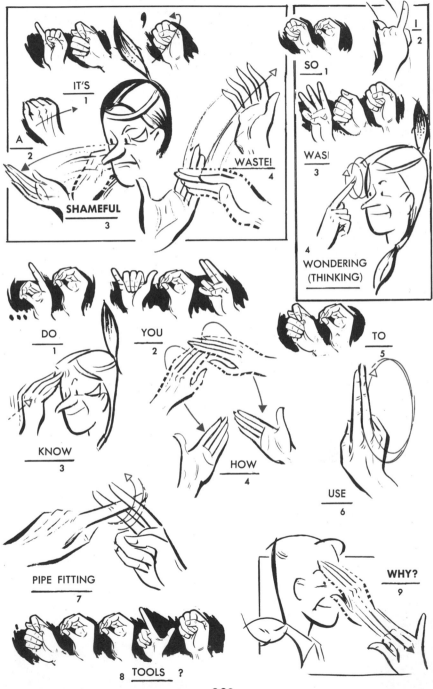

IT'S
1

A
2

SHAMEFUL
3

WASTE!
4

SO
1

I
2

WASH
3

WONDERING
(THINKING)
4

DO
1

YOU
2

KNOW
3

HOW
4

TO
5

USE
6

PIPE FITTING
7

TOOLS ?
8

WHY?
9

233

PLEASE
1

(See page 107)
2

WHAT
3

"PEA-WEE"
4

RAISED
5

AND
6

GREW
7

IN
8

HIS
9

GARDEN
10

234

Index

238

FAIL 24
FAILURE 24
FAIR (ness) 62
FAITH 53
FALL (season) 143
FALL (ing) 68
FALL BEHIND 10
FALL FOR HER (fall for him) 181
FALLING IN LOVE 225
FALSE FRIEND 64
FALSEHOOD 99
FAMILY 88
FAMOUS 57
FANCY 228
FAR 227
FAR INTO THE NIGHT 110
FARMER 131
FARMLAND 146
FASCINATE 15
FAST 30
FASTER 203
FAT 121
FAT (slang) 177
FATHER 89, 173
FAVOR 139
FEAR 67
FEARFUL 60
FED UP 181
FEEBLE MINDED 14
FEED (ing) 101
FEEL 44, 210
FEEL HURT 48
FEEL BAD 46
FEEL FULL 103
FEEL GOOD 46
FELL 210
FELT 44, 210
FEMALE 89, 133
FENCE (yard) 114
FEVER 121
FEW DAYS, IN A 74
FEW DAYS AGO 74
FEW SECONDS AGO 73
FIGHT 49
FIGURE 169
FILE 32
FILLED 62, 148
FILTH 63, 167
FILTHY 63, 167
FINALLY 208
FIND 18, 200
FINE 66, 210
FINE (charge) 136
FINGER SPELLER 184

FINISH (ed) 24, 26
FIRE 151
FIRED 41
FISH 227
FISH BAIT 157
FISHING 157
FIRST 202
FIX 152
FLAG 153
FLAME 151
FLEA 168
FLIRTING 225
FLOOR 111
FLOWER 114
FLU 118
FLY 149, 168
FLYING 203
FOLLOW 40
FOLLOWERS 95
FOOD 100
FOOL 99
FOOLISH 47
FOOT (measure) 86
FOOTBALL 158
FOR 210
FORBID 59
FORBIDDEN 59
FOR INSTANCE 58
FORCE 137
FORECAST 145
FOREST 144
FORGET 17
FORGIVE (ness) 17, 95
FORK 112
FOX 165
FRACTIONS 82, 83
FRANCE 154
FRANKLY 224
FREE 63, 136
FREEDOM 136
FREEZE 103
FRENCH 154
FRENCH FRIED 102
FRESH 105
FRIDAY 76
FRIED 102
FRIEND (ly) 56
FRIENDSHIP 56
FRIGHTEN 48
FROG 167
FROM 7
FRONT 193
FROZEN 103
FRUIT 107
FULL 62, 148
FUN 50
FUNERAL 123

FUNNY 50, 191

GAIN 126
GALLAUDET 23
GAS 148
GATHERING (meeting) 139
GENTLEMAN 90
GENTLENESS 50
GERMAN 155
GERMANY 155
GET (got) 24, 160
GETTING OFF 149
GHOST 92
GIFT 28
GIRL 88
GIVE 28
GIVE ATTENTION TO 40
GIVE UP 39
GLAD 200
GLASS 111, 112
GLASSES 118
GLISTENING 63
GLOBE (earth) 142
GLOOMY 49
GLORY 94
GO 28, 35, 208
GOAL 71
GOAT 166
GO ALONE (went alone) 32
GOD 92
GOING 35
GOGGLES 157
GOLD 149
GOLF 157
GONE (slang) 179
GOODBYE 49
GOOD IMPRESSION 46
GOOD JUDGMENT 46
GONE 9
GOSSIP (ing) 29
GOVERNMENT 134
GOVERNOR 134
GRADUATE 22
GRANDFATHER 88
GRANDMOTHER 8
GRAPES 107
GRAVE 123
GRAVY 102
GRAY 65
GREASE 102
GREATEST 57
GREECE 156
GREEK 156
GREEN 70
GREEN (slang) 178
GRIEF 225

244

245